Also from the Author

Choices: A Novel
The Adventures of Alex and Angelo

VOYAGERS
INTO THE
UNKNOWN

RUCHIRA KHANNA

BALBOA.
PRESS

A DIVISION OF HAY HOUSE

Balboa Press books may be ordered through booksellers or by contacting:

Balboa Press
A Division of Hay House
1663 Liberty Drive
Bloomington, IN 47403
www.balboapress.com
1 (877) 407-4847

Because of the dynamic nature of the Internet, any web addresses or links contained in this book may have changed since publication and may no longer be valid. The views expressed in this work are solely those of the author and do not necessarily reflect the views of the publisher, and the publisher hereby disclaims any responsibility for them.

The author of this book does not dispense medical advice or prescribe the use of any technique as a form of treatment for physical, emotional, or medical problems without the advice of a physician, either directly or indirectly. The intent of the author is only to offer information of a general nature to help you in your quest for emotional and spiritual well-being. In the event you use any of the information in this book for yourself, which is your constitutional right, the author and the publisher assume no responsibility for your actions.

Any people depicted in stock imagery provided by Thinkstock are models, and such images are being used for illustrative purposes only.
Certain stock imagery © Thinkstock.

Print information available on the last page.

ISBN: 978-1-5043-4546-0 (sc)
ISBN: 978-1-5043-4547-7 (e)

Library of Congress Control Number: 2015919739

Balboa Press rev. date: 01/08/2016

Contents

Arrival of the Birds 1

The Heart Wants What it Wants. 19

Blank Slate 22

Live While We're Young 27

Shake it Off. 35

The Long and Winding Road 52

Wide Awake 68

Take Care 84

Say Something 99

A New Day Has Come 103

Forever Until Tomorrow 114

Night Changes 120

No More Second Chances. 125

You and I 128

Story of My Life 132

All of Me. 134

Part of Me. 143

Set Fire to the Rain 147

Arrival of the Birds

Dawn had risen over the historic Indian town of Agra. Agra was a city of monuments, which stood tall, their unmatched grandeur telling of their long and fascinating history. The morning air was filled with the sounds of roosters calling, birds chirping, and morning prayers and salutations. Dogs and cows were being hustled through the streets and errand boys on bicycles hurried along to their respective chores and deliveries.

Amidst this vibrant chaos, a man in his late thirties with an athletic physique, broad shoulders, and unkempt black hair was briefing his colleague in a quiet, affable tone. He held a bunch of papers in his hand, and the other man nodded obediently as he glanced through them, making notes on the pad in his hands. "So, are you all set?" inquired Raj, the black-haired man.

"I think so," replied the other man confidently, as he took his seat behind the wheel of a mini-bus.

"Call me if you have any questions, Albert. You know where to reach me," added Raj as he shut the door of the driver's seat, giving his driver two thumbs up. Albert started the engine quickly and began to roll away from the curb. He was abruptly halted by a sharp knock on the door of the vehicle. The driver slammed on the brakes and looked to see who was doing the hammering. Raj reappeared on the other side of the glass with blank boards and a sharpie. Albert opened the door and reached out for the additional items. "Write the names of my birds on these planks. It will be easier for them to spot you," explained Raj.

"Birds?" inquired Albert with a confused expression.

"Sure, Birds. Since they will fly back to where they are coming from in a week's time."

"Aha! Yes, boss!" Albert winked and started his journey.

After driving continuously for four and a half hours, Albert finally reached Delhi Airport. He glanced through the various itineraries and wrote a name down in bold letters, IRA ADDISON. Then he went to the arrival gate of the international flights and held the plank high so that the disembarking passengers could read it.

A few minutes ticked by. "Hi," a female passenger waved and walked towards him. "Raj?"

"No... uhhm... yes?" Albert paused awkwardly, "I am Albert. I'm the driver for 'Raj Touristry.' I will take you to Agra, where the tour will begin." He extended his hand towards her. Ira shook hands with him, placing her glasses over her tired eyes while pulling back her unkempt golden hair that was gleaming in the sun. Her thin, petite frame was only thirty years old, yet she had the delicate fragility of someone much older.

"How was your journey, Ira?" Albert inquired as he helped her load her luggage.

Ira pondered his question, thinking back on her journey.

She had checked in her luggage and waited impatiently with a heavy heart to board that plane. Sitting in the lounge area, she had scrutinized the expressions of the other passengers to see if she could tell why they were going to New Delhi, India. Most of her fellow passengers had either radiated joy or were too engrossed in their laptops or smartphones to show any expression at all. The latter group was probably on some sort of business trip. The happy faces of the others, however, had brought forth a cry of pain from her heart. Their joyful expressions clashed hurtfully with her own feelings.

Why me? Where did I go wrong? As these words echoed in her mind, she had realized that tears were rolling down her cheeks. She quickly wiped them away with her shirtsleeve and pulled her shades down over her eyes. She was a strong woman. She couldn't break down like this. It would ruin her reputation. This salty flood was only allowed within the confines of the four bare walls of her house. House, not home. Her home had been swept away when someone walked out of her life, ripped her heart out, and left her to pick up the pieces alone.

"Flight 762 to New Delhi, now boarding," the flight attendant announced. Ira pulled her frail, weak body off the seat and moved toward the embarkation line. She noticed a businesswoman in front of her who was well dressed and fashionably styled. She used to have such a well-toned physique and well-put-together appearance, but not anymore. She'd taken such care and pride in her daily "getting ready" regimen. Her mornings consisted of waking up at the brink of dawn and planning every minute of her day in minute detail. This set her up to achieve whatever she had tasked herself with, leading up to the minute at which she'd plunk herself onto the couch in complete satisfaction next to her man, Pete, who was just the opposite.

They had been the poster couple for the saying, "opposites attract." Still, they made an incredible team when it came to sharing their emotions and feelings. She always felt that she could talk to him about anything that had bothered her at work or elsewhere during the day. He had a laid back way of approaching problems, which contrasted with how Ira was very aggressive and rash in her actions. Her motto was, "If not now, then never." Pete warned her sometimes about the repercussions of that attitude, but since she had felt that time was on her side, she had paid him little heed.

That was one of our main problems, she thought with sadness as she shifted in her seat, trying to get comfortable. She buckled up and pulled off her shades to take one final look outside. She hoped that when she returned home, she would have a new perspective on everything. Then a soft nudge against her shoulder reminded her that she wasn't alone. She whirled around to look at the passenger next to her. "Excuse me," a young, well-dressed man said politely as he sidled into his seat, awkwardly juggling an armful of gadgets.

Ira nodded and gave him a quick smile. Then she made a point of focusing her attention on a random magazine from the seat back pocket in front of her. She absent-mindedly flipped through the magazine, trying to avoid having to make small talk with her neighbor.

"So, you into technology too?" A loud voice startled her. Annoyed, she frowned and whirled around to glare at the man sitting next to her. But he wasn't the one who had interrupted her thoughts. It was another man, who was sitting two seats away from her. He had an eager look on his face as he pointed at the magazine she was holding.

Her face turned red as she looked down, realizing that she had a tech magazine in her hands. She shrugged her shoulders as she replied, "Yeah, kinda... not really. Just looking to see if there are any interesting new iPhone accessories?"

His face fell, and he nodded politely. Then he turned his attention back to his laptop. She closed the magazine and placed it back into the seat pocket in front of her. She sighed and ran her hand through her long blonde hair. Her once soft tresses felt brittle to the touch, and she promised herself that she'd see to fixing that when she got back from this trip. She smiled wryly, remembering how she used to jump with excitement at seeing any new brand of conditioner on the store shelves. That time was long gone, along with Pete. He'd taken away all her passions, everything she adored, and even her zeal for living when he walked out on her.

Why? Ira asked her heart, but it gave no answer. She blinked back fresh tears and turned her gaze to the window. The rest of her journey was a relatively quiet affair since Ira wanted no business with anybody. The polite, well-dressed man next to her tried to start up several conversations, but she always shot him down with a curt "yes" or "no" answer. After about an hour of trying, he took the hint, pulled out his headphones, and kept to himself.

The hours ticked by slowly as Ira's attention shifted restlessly back and forth from her dark window shade to her TV screen. Her mind relentlessly paced down the airplane aisle and back again in search of some answer to her anxiety—anything that would help her calm down. She desperately wanted to put the pieces of her life back together again, but she just couldn't find out where those darn pieces were hidden. Her constant fidgeting and shaking eventually aroused the curiosity of her co-passenger. He eyed her every now and then, but she pretended not to notice. At one point during her fidgeting, she scratched her wrist against the window, peeling a bit of skin off. She immediately pulled a tube of Vaseline from her purse to moisturize it. Whenever she touched her wrists, she was reminded of the time she'd deliberately cut those veins, laying in a pool of her own blood on the floor. She had let everything go. She'd succumbed to the loneliness and the apprehension and fear that resulted from being alone.

Then a few hours later, she regained consciousness to realize she was in a hospital with clean sheets beneath her and a plethora of nurses and doctors attending her. A couple of counseling sessions later, she was given the green light to carry on with her life. She always wished her scars could have been truly healed by those therapy sessions, but the psychologist made the wound deeper with her probing questions, such as, "What is life, and what is the meaning of it?" Ira's blood thickened as she pondered these questions, and the dark red liquid refused to flow out any further from her body. On the outside, she was considered "healed" but on the inside, her scars felt just as raw as the day she'd tried to end her life.

On the day of her discharge, she was prescribed iron and multivitamins since she had lost so much blood. They had even tried to give her a transfusion. She was shocked to be alive and also curious as to how she'd gotten to the hospital. Her discharge nurse, a kind woman named Kathy, had looked through her records and answered with a pout as she scratched her elbow, "The man who brought you to us identified himself as Edwin Garmin. Do you know him?"

Ira frowned, confused. "Edwin who?"

Kathy's voice betrayed her irritation. "Garmin."

Ira offered a conciliatory smile. "I am sure I'll remember eventually. I'm just drained."

The nurse chuckled. "I must say, though, he was anxious about you when you were wheeled in. I'm surprised you don't have any idea who he is."

Ira lowered her head in embarrassment. Her life had revolved around Pete and only Pete. After he left, the whole world suddenly seemed to be draped by a thick white sheet that prevented her from seeing anything. It was unlikely that she'd be able to identify anybody that she had met since then.

"You should look around your neighborhood. I'm told he lives in the same building as you," Kathy added nonchalantly, then turned her back to Ira to answer a phone call.

Ira folded her prescription and carefully placed it in her bag as she headed out to her waiting cab. Who was Edwin Garmin? She did not care less, cause at that point she needed to jump-start her life before she would go searching for some Edwin.

A gentle voice brought her back to the airplane. "Miss Addison, what would you like today? Chicken or steak?"

Ira blinked, glancing up at the pretty young stewardess who was wheeling the meal cart down the aisle. "I'll have the chicken, please." She tied her hair back and lowered her meal tray. The aroma from her tray drifted towards her and made her stomach rumble. Only then did she realize how hungry she had been. In no time, she gobbled up her meal, leaving not a single morsel. She suddenly felt a lot better. Maybe she had let her thoughts and her hunger get the best of her. Feeling a slight bit of food coma coming on, Ira pulled out her cardigan and blanket and snuggled up like a cat in her seat. Her light snores initially shocked and surprised her co-passenger, but after a small chuckle, he adapted to them.

Even though her body was tired exhausted, Ira's heart ached for her destination. So every now and again, she would wake up to eagerly check the map on the seat back in front of her. She watched as the tiny plane depicted on the screen's map inched closer and closer to Delhi. Then after a minute or two of sharp look at the map on the screen to check their whereabouts she would inevitably drift back into a slumber mode but would take a few minutes to calm her restlessness.

A few hours later, the pilot announced they would be landing shortly at the Delhi Airport. At this news, Ira jumped up and reached under her seat to grab her purse.

The man next to her raised his eyebrows and snorted. "Whoa! Buckle up, lady. We have not even landed yet!"

She paused to give him a dirty look and then continued to do as she had planned. She picked up her bag and took out her phone and charger. She brushed her hair while she read a particular visiting card over and over again. She sensed the young man next to her, who was not being particularly polite at the moment, reading the card over her shoulder, and she changed its position slightly so it would be harder for him to see.

"Meeting someone special in Delhi?" he asked, giving her a playful nudge.

"Yes, I am seeing Raj. He is going to change my world and my perception," she answered curtly.

His eyes widened. "Are you sure you know what you are doing?" his tone was kind but concerned.

She nodded, then put the card in the pocket of her jeans and checked the percentage of charge on her phone. Her silent treatment had been given to many prior to her departure to India, so she was getting pretty good at it. She'd refused to comment or clarify to either her parents or her best friend, Melissa, and she'd been accused of being too stubborn for her own sake. She'd gotten tired of living under the weight of self-pity and wanted a life of her own. She wanted to fly again, but her wings were bruised so badly that even her own licks could not heal them. When she'd boarded her flight from Portland, no one had come to see her off, and she was surprisingly okay with that. Playing deaf to her co-passenger was a piece of cake compared to ignoring her loved ones.

So, after an awkward pause, he added, "Well, good luck to you, then."

"Excuse me, Ira? Ma'am? Is everything alright?" Albert's concerned voice snapped her out of her train of thought, and she met his eyes with bewilderment. She flushed, realizing how deep she had been in thought and wondering how long she had been non-responsive.

She hastily replied, "I am fine."

Albert smiled, offering her some refreshment, to which she did not hesitate. *Blame it on the warm weather.* After a couple of minutes, he wrote DARCI & LENNARD JENSEN on a white board. Then he made sure that Ira was comfortable and safe on the bus before heading with the plank in hand towards the arrival gate of another international flight.

When Darci and Lennard Jensen had boarded their flight from Copenhagen, life around them was bustling with vigor and excitement, since the aircraft mostly consisted of high school children on a school trip. Lennard found the teenagers' constant chitter chatter very irritating in the lounge area. While walking towards the aircraft, he asked to be seated near the window, to which Darci promptly agreed since she knew her husband well. An incident between them had caused him to mature faster than normal for his age, and even though they were only in their late twenties, he preferred a quiet life more suited for an older man. He was never found without a book by his side. In contrast, his wife Darci was happy to take the aisle seat. She wanted a good view of the other passengers, and hopefully, there would be some fun and interesting people to converse with during the lengthy journey to come.

As soon as Lennard parked himself in his window seat, he buried his nose in his book. Darci looked around eagerly, trying to make eye contact with the teenagers. However, they were too busy amongst themselves to pay any heed to her smiles or side comments, which she would find extremely funny and giggle over to herself. She kept waiting for a response, but none was to come. Darci eventually realized this, and crestfallen glanced over at Lennard, who was entirely absorbed in his book. She peeked at the cover, and then poked him playfully to get his attention. Irritated, he looked at her with raised eyebrows.

"Is there a problem?" he asked with a nasty tone in his voice.

She swallowed her emotions, but her moist eyes gave it away. She quickly turned the other way, timidly answering, "No, never mind, it's nothing." Annoyed and hurt, Darci got up to go to the restroom.

In that two by two-foot confine, she found peace. Her tears knew no boundaries, and she let them flow. Every time Lennard snapped at her and denied her the love and companionship she craved, she cursed herself for staying with him. She wanted to escape, but then she started to feel like the foolish child he often accused her of being. "Oh grow up, Darci!" he would exclaim when she begged for his attention.

Their marriage had been heading in a downhill spiral. Yet, she respected him for standing up for her, in spite of the many who indicted her. A single moment came flashing back to her, and she felt all her anger melt away. She turned the tap to get some water running and splashed it on her face with force. "You silly girl," she muttered to herself. "Do not lose hope. Just give him time. He loves you. This trip will do wonders for your relationship. Just be glad that he agreed to come along," she reassured herself with a deep breath. Then she pulled a mini cosmetic bag from her sweater pocket. She applied thick black liner along her upper lash line, added some color to her lips and her cheeks, and quickly brushed her short brown hair, which always tended to curl up at the ends.

Filled with a newfound assurance, she walked back to her seat, where Lennard had momentarily put away his book in order to begin eating his dinner. Upon noticing her, he looked up from his dinner tray and snapped, "Where have you been?"

Darci smiled and responded mischievously, "Why, I was in the restroom, dearest. Did you actually miss me?"

Lennard ignored her comment, giving her an expressionless look. "The stewardess brought your food. Since I had no idea where you were, I told her to take it back." Then he resumed eating as if nothing had happened.

Darci was stunned. Then she was relieved when she saw Lennard reach up and push the call button to summon the attendant. The stewardess approached promptly and turned off the glowing light above their heads, asking, "How may I help you?"

Darci quickly responded, "May I have my dinner service now please?"

"Oh no! You did not get your food tray? How come? Did you have a special request?" she checked out the seat number and pulled out a paper from her pocket.

"No, no special requests. I was in the restroom when you handed my husband his tray," she responded with anxiety.

"Sheesh! Now we are out of dinner trays."

Lennard was quick to interject in a serious and commanding tone, "I specifically urged the attendant who handed me my food to keep her plate. Why was her dinner given away?"

Darci was relieved again to hear him speak up on her behalf. She fidgeted with her wedding ring as the two of them spoke. The attendant hastily apologized. "Let me check if the first class has any extra food to spare." Before Lennard could reply, she took off briskly in the direction of the pilot's cockpit. Darci smiled at her husband and squeezed his arm to indicate her thanks. But Lennard was in a different mood altogether and did not reciprocate. In times like this, she felt that their eight-year age difference significantly affected their relationship, especially when she wanted to be playful and he wanted to be serious. However, she could not forget those early days of their union when they would just pack their toothbrushes and go on long drives together. Needless to say, they would give each other undivided attention back then since no books or electronic gadgets were involved in those trips.

She smiled and blushed at her memories, putting her arms around herself comfortingly. She still got excited goosebumps whenever she thought back on the early part of their relationship. Eventually, she returned to the present moment, and looked around for the stewardess, anxiously anticipating her food. Luckily, a few minutes later, the attendant returned with a tray and a smile, placing the food next to Darci. Darci savored her food with sincere appreciation, finishing it quickly. Once the meal was finished, she wrapped her petite, five-foot-tall body in a blanket, dozing off.

Lennard continued to read. He would occasionally check on her and adjust her covers as she haphazardly shifted from one position to another.

As he adjusted her blanket, Lennard realized that Darci not only had a habit to move randomly in her sleep but also when awake. She was a ball of constant energy, flitting from one idea to another, a free spirit to the core. He reflected on his relationship with her. He loved her eternally, but her flighty and spontaneous personality irritated him endlessly. Just then, her hand flew into his lap. He nodded with a compassionate smile, as he gently picked up her hand to place it back on her side.

Looking down, he was distracted by her fingers, which used to bring relief to his aching muscles during her massages. He spent many hours a day on the computer at work, and his hands were often rheumatic and sore as a result. The relief from her gentle massages was beyond words, and at times, her loving touch would turn into an eventful evening. The sounds of laughter filled his ears as he wandered down memory lane of those latter parts of the day, in which their bodies vigorously intertwined until the first ray of sunshine touched upon their windowsill. He looked out the plane window with her hand in his and reflected on those years that made everything seem so magical. He had never dreamt that there would be a day to come when his relationship perched on the brink of a steep hill and could go sliding down into a dungeon of despair at any moment.

He knew that he had to do something. His reluctance to make a decision about whether to stay together was hurting both of them. His eyes grew moist as a certain memory returned to haunt him, and he sighed and placed Darci's hand back in her seat. To avoid any more troubling thoughts, he resumed reading. It served as a useful distraction from the thoughts that he was scared to face.

The pilot's announcement woke Darci up. She looked at Lennard with sleepy eyes. He had not slept a wink and was still busy reading. She stretched herself energetically, making Lennard a little irritated. He struggled to dodge her waving hands. She did not care and continued to spread anyways. "I am so excited about this trip. Aren't you?" she asked curiously as she placed her arms around him.

Lennard gave her a sidelong look and replied in a flat tone, "I really hope your friend was right about this trip, and it's worth our time and money."

"Oh! Yes, it will be, dear!" as she moved her hands lower, encircling his waist and placing her head on his chest. Lennard sat cold and still, crossing his fingers in the hope that she was right.

Lennard approached Albert and introduced himself. Darci introduced herself enthusiastically and smiled at the driver. After exchanging a few pleasantries, they walked towards their vehicle. Ira was introduced to them, and the four sat enjoying occasional sips of cold iced tea to quench their thirst. It was already a hot Delhi morning. Before they knew it, Albert had to put the pedal to the metal to fetch CARL BAKER in time. Albert stepped down to get him with his name on a freshly-written plank. He displayed the board, and soon there was a tap on his shoulder.

"Raj?"

"No... I am Albert. I will drive you to Agra where you will meet Raj," Albert clarified.

Carl was wiping the sweat off his forehead as he walked with the driver towards the bus.

"How was your trip, Carl?"

"Huh! Nothing unusual. Glad it's over and I have reached my destination," replied the tourist with a relieved expression as he recounted the trip in his mind.

Carl Baker had boarded his flight in Frankfurt. His fragile yet fit seventy-five-year-old body had seen it all... he reminisced on the ups and down of life and the empire he had built along with it. The stewardess helped him with his coat and carry-on baggage to which he was delighted to hand over. His smile revealed the laugh lines and wrinkles. He'd long ago given up on Botox injections. Even though his hands were manicured, the crinkles along his fingers told it all. He was happy to seat himself in a comfortable and spacious first class seat and sip his champagne. He looked out the window and wondered if he had activated the security alarm after bolting all his windows and doors. His palatial estate had witnessed his two failed marriages, and his son had left him too since he wanted a lot more than his father was able to give. Today, he had to secure his mansion, and the fact that he was leaving his multi-million dollar property behind along with his business, filled him with anxiety and dread, to say the least. He smirked at his destiny. Even after working for fifty-five years, and creating enough wealth to feed his descendants and their families; he could not successfully build a family that would stay beside him. The concept of love did not sit right with him. He even pitied himself as he took the last sip from his champagne flute.

"Hi, Carl!" Carl was quick to turn around. He loved company but just could not understand why people didn't stick around him for very long. He looked in the direction of the voice and the welcome sight of an old friend brought a smile to his face. He lit up, placed his empty glass on the table and got up to give his friend a hug.

"What a surprise, Tony!" he exclaimed. Tony smiled and took the seat next to him.

"What business takes you to Delhi, my friend? You never travel to Asia!" asked a curious Tony.

Carl was stunned by his honesty. He paused and chose his words wisely. "Hmmm... Just some important business that I couldn't ignore any longer," he replied, hoping that Tony wouldn't delve any further. Tony was his old schoolmate. They often saw each other at alumni gatherings. He was a professor at Frankfurt University of Music and Arts and even though his status and finances were no match for Carl's, he was a happy and content man. Carl often wondered why a man of Tony's talent and intellect didn't pursue a more lucrative career, but he respected him nonetheless.

"How is Barbara?" asked his curious classmate.

Carl scratched his head, smoothing a few stray strands of his freshly dyed hair back into place. He sighed and replied with remorse, "We are separated."

"Oh! I am very sorry to hear that," Tony looked down awkwardly, then pulled some papers from his briefcase and shuffled through them, pretending to have important business to take care of. He was a true intellectual; however

he'd never had a very delicate touch when it came to matters of the heart. He worried about Carl but really didn't know what to say to make him feel better. His university was sponsoring his trip to Delhi so that he could gather some data with regards to music and instruments, but he hoped that he would have some spare time to spend with his old friend so that he might attempt to brighten his spirits. Carl had always been the life of the party. Tony wondered what he could do to cheer his friend up. Maybe a drink would help?

Carl always made it a point to showcase his power, along with his possessions. Watching his friend struggle awkwardly for words, he quickly rebooted himself, "Nah! Don't worry about it at all, Tony. We parted on reasonably good terms. I've told myself that it's for the best," he announce with as much false bravado as he could muster, giving his pal a hearty thump on the back.

Tony looked up from his papers and smiled. The old Carl was back. He breathed a silent sigh of relief. "How about another glass of champagne? Let's toast to that!" he suggested.

Carl nodded in agreement and reached for the call button. But just then they were interrupted by the pilot's announcement of taking off. Once the plane had reached cruising altitude, Carl excused himself to use the restroom. As he got up, his eyes caught the sight of the ring on his friend's left finger. He was filled immediately with a strangely envious feeling, but he pushed it out of his mind as quickly as he could, hurrying down the aisle to the restroom. He quickly shut himself inside and locked the door. He took a deep breath, and murmured to his reflection in the mirror, "Damn you, Carl! You handsome hunk. How much I love you. But, dammit! Today you are losing! You have nothing of true worth to showcase to Tony, who can't even afford a ticket abroad! Who would have thought the tables would have turned like this?" he chuckled ruefully. He reached into his pocket and pulled out some eye drops and a travel-size bottle of cologne. He freshened up, lightened his bladder, and walked back to his seat feeling like a new man. Perhaps there would even be a pretty woman on this flight to distract him. After all, he was back on the market again… why not have a bit of fun?

Tony greeted him with a warm nod.

"So, enough about me. How have you been, my friend?" asked Carl. "I am assuming you are traveling on the department's dime?" he added with a saucy wink.

Tony was quick to apprehend, "Yes, I am, Carl. As you know, a professor's salary doesn't typically allow him to travel first class," he replied with a crooked smile. "I am headed to Delhi to research Indian music and instruments. Much of my time leading up to this was focused on preparations for this trip. But aside from that, my son is in the United States on a work visa, working at a Biotech company. Meanwhile, myself and my sweet Donna are enjoying the fruits of freedom!" he added, playfully kissing his ring on the finger.

Carl's heart sunk again at this reminder of happy matrimony. He was not used to seeing others happier than he, and frankly, it made him uncomfortable. He reclined his seat, but that did not satisfy him. "How about that drink now?" he suggested, hitting the call button over his head. "What kind of service do you have here?" snapped an irritated Carl when the stewardess appeared.

"Excuse me, Sir?" came her polite reply.

"It has been nearly an hour since the plane took off, and my glass is empty. I haven't even received a snack, much less any food service since prior to taking off. What are you ladies doing over there? Playing cards?" asked Carl mockingly, and glancing sidelong at Tony, hoping that he would join in the fun. Surprisingly, Tony was focusing on his papers, pretending not to hear any of it. This irritated Carl even more. He got up, pushed past the stewardess, and began walking towards the galley. She gasped, and then hurried after him.

Tony could hear some angry voices coming from the galley, but they quickly subsided. Carl returned proudly to his seat with a crooked smile and a glass of red wine. He shook some pills into his hand, swallowed them with a generous gulp of wine, and was soon snoring loudly. Tony glanced around and noticed that their fellow passengers and the stewardesses looked immensely relieved to see him in that state. Tony shook his head and muttered, "Carl has not changed a bit! His negativity will swallow him whole one of these days..."

A few hours later, Carl awoke with a refreshed smile. "Feeling better, Carl?" inquired Tony.

"Oh! Yes. I badly needed that nap. The last few days were tough for me. I had to bring my business to a halt and make it so that a delegate could handle my business while I am out of the country. Business can really take a toll on one's mind, huh?" he looked at Tony expectantly.

Tony felt the urge to ask his friend a question but bit his tongue. Instead, he smiled and just said, "Well, I am glad you got some rest, buddy. Sounds like you did need it indeed."

The two men sat in relatively peaceful silence for the rest of the flight, enjoying the delicious dinner service and having a couple drinks. Tony focused on his research while Carl entertained himself with a movie and extra liquor until the announcement of arrival to Delhi was made. Then Carl's anxiety kicked in again. He finished his glass in a single gulp and began to fidget anxiously. He pulled out a visiting card from his pocket, and read it over carefully, murmuring under his breath, "This better be good and worth my time and money. Or else I will sue that bloody lawyer, Bushnell."

Albert and Carl walked briskly to the van, and Carl was introduced to the other passengers. Albert checked the watch. "We have one more tour member to pick up. She is a local to this area. Then we will head to the city where your tour will begin," he announced as he started the engine.

The last tour member, Asha, wrapped her slippers in a mesh bag before placing them in her suitcase. She scanned her room one last time, then zipped her bag, locked it and dragged it to the door. Then she placed her purse next to it. She took a quick shower and then glanced at the clock as she briskly toweled herself off.

"Hurry up, Mrs. Menon, you have only thirty minutes left to get ready!" came her helper's urgent request from another room.

Asha nodded and replied, "Yes! I'm almost done!" She grimaced with anxiety and whispered to herself, "Deadlines still make me sweat. Ughh!" Soon, she was pulling up her pants, and throwing a blouse over herself. She quickly combed her short white hair and grabbed her sneakers. Age was catching up with her body. Ever since she had turned sixty, her body was getting more and more fragile. Then the doorbell rang. "Aha! Just in time," she said with a smile, and shouted out, "Kamala!"

A lady clad in Indian attire opened the door and greeted the driver outside, who addressed himself as Albert. Kamala pointed at the bag, which he promptly picked up. Asha came out of her bedroom, put the purse on her shoulder, gave a quick hug to Kamala, and walked out the door. Albert greeted her and helped her into the vehicle, where she encountered some friendly-looking but unfamiliar faces. They introduced themselves, and Asha took the seat diagonal to the driver.

"We will reach Agra in about four hours depending on traffic. There are some light refreshments next to you. Please feel free to indulge in them," offered Albert. Then they took off.

Asha looked back to catch the last glimpse of her home. Then she smiled and faced forward, excited about her one-week mini vacation. She had been so busy getting all her stuff in order for the trip, that feeding herself had been the last thing on her to-do list. She quickly gulped some cold tea and took a grateful bite of a sandwich from one of the trays. Soothing and melodious music was being played over the speakers of the mini bus and Asha gazed out the tinted windows as they drove. She watched the people they passed as they beat along the daily grind of life, all going about their respective business. She took a deep breath and allowed the icy cold air of the air-conditioned car fill her lungs.

I am blessed to have led such a good life… she thought to herself. My children are well settled abroad. My pension keeps my house running, and my small income works as my savings. Although my heart will always miss Abhay, I shall continue to live the rest of my life in accord with karma and destiny. She looked down at the lines of her palm.

"People your age should be going on a religious pilgrimage. So, what makes you take this journey to Agra, Ma'am?" asked the curious driver, eying Asha with gentle curiosity.

Asha was taken aback for a few seconds by his bold question and was tempted to answer snappily. Instead, she paused for a few seconds, then chuckled at the young driver's curiosity and replied, "Nowhere does it say that grey-haired folk ought only to visit holy places. Besides, this is a refresher course for me in terms of getting to know about life and how I should embrace it for my remaining years."

Albert nodded in agreement. "Raj is splendid at that. Many people from abroad come to get a taste of this," he replied with confidence.

Asha felt proud of her choice of words after hearing the latter and devoured the rest of her sandwich. "I hope my booking in the hotel is confirmed, Albert," she asked between bites.

"Yes, ma'am. Raj sees to all the bookings himself once payment is done. You will be residing in the Taj hotel until your tour with Raj ends," he said with a smile.

"Hmmm... That is most interesting!" replied Asha in delight. Her fellow tourists were snoozing, with the exception of one. Ira's eyes were glued outside the window. She previously had no clue that Raj Touristry was so famous. This made her, even more, proud of her choice and selection. The melodic background music was making Asha's eyelids heavy too, and after assuming a relaxing position, she dozed off.

The Heart Wants What it Wants

After giving instructions to Albert, Raj decided to take a nap, since he knew the day ahead of him would be a very busy one. He was awakened by the doorbell. He took a big yawn and stretched his arms out as if to embrace the heavens, but instead he caught a tangle of cobwebs. He was slow to answer the door since he knew who it was already. He hastily wiped his cobweb-covered hands on his shirt, and went to the kitchen to fetch an empty container. Then he opened the door and was greeted by a tall, husky guy with a big mustache. Scratching his head, Raj asked him, "Where is Shyam Babu?"

To which the mustachioed man replied, "Oh he left for his village. There was an emergency."

Raj shook his head disapprovingly.

The milkman pretended not to notice, and continued, "From now on, I will be your new milkman," he said with a smile.

Raj intervened, "I hope your milk will have less water and more milk? Can I trust you?"

"Oh yes, absolutely, Raj-jee. I will be delivering milk to your whole apartment complex. How could I possibly cheat so many of you?" but he had a mischievous twinkle in his eye.

"Glad to hear that. I will pay you next month, since your friend,

Shyam Babu had taken an advance for this month before commencing on his emergency route."

"Oh yes, Shyam told me about that," he replied meekly.

Raj took the milk and shut the door. There was a world atlas affixed to the back of his door, on which many cities had been circled. He took a minute to admire his atlas, then grinned and started to get ready for work. Raj was a tour guide. He loved history, landmarks, and monuments. A post-graduate in economics, he decided not to use his degree, but instead to show the grandeur of this great city to tourists from all over the world. After all, following the heart and its wants is the way to live! His passion for history had guided him to start his own tour company, Raj Touristry, and his tour style had a special touch that attracted people from all over the world. However, he ran his business solely on word of mouth and refused to advertise it on social media, thereby limiting it to only a handful of tourists.

He opened the door of his office, which had a sign that read, "Raj Touristry." He heard his phone ring. He quickly answered. "Hello? Oh, Hi Meera! Nice to hear your voice. How have you been? How was your cousin's wedding?" asked enthusiastic Raj, hardly giving Meera a chance to breathe between those questions. He realized the number of queries he had put forward and paused for her to answer. After hearing her replies, he continued with zeal, "Oh! Great. So the four rooms are confirmed. Please make sure a table for six is also booked under my name. You know the drill, Meera," he said with intensity, and finally prior to hanging up, he added sweetly, "I have missed you."

He looked at his watch, and quickly performed his morning prayer ritual, lighting a stick of incense and acknowledging all the pictures of the Gods displayed in his shop. Once he finished, he started working on his paperwork and calling various places to double check their reservations with Raj Touristry. He just could not tolerate any errors in his tour itineraries, especially when people were traveling from far and wide to pay a visit to Indian history and delve into the world of the 18th century.

His goal was not only to share these wonders but also to help people to reflect on their own lives and personal goals. He didn't want this to be hampered by standing in the heat too long or any other inconveniences. The motto of his tour business was, "Discover Yourself Amidst History!"

Raj always aimed his trips to be comfortable and hassle-free for his tour members. He assured them the time and space to reflect on their struggles and get the most value for their money. After all, that was what he charged travelers for. Any normal guide could simply show them around the city, but his distinguished motto helped change people's lives for the better. And he had been working on his references for the past eight years. He was genuinely proud of what he had accomplished because his tours were life changing for his travelers and had given him fond memories and good friends in return.

He got up from his desk, put his papers into orderly piles, and pulled down the shutters of his shop. He headed home for a quick shower and change of clothes. The month of August offered hot and sultry weather, and that could make even the locals sweat. After showering, he put some talcum powder over his chest and underarms and dabbed on a bit of an expensive aftershave that had been a gift from one of his former travelers. As he was pulling on his jeans and sliding into his favorite dress shirt, he felt blessed to have made such wonderful acquaintances that refused to forget him. He admired himself in his dressing table mirror. His six-foot-tall physique was lean and toned. His big, round brown eyes sparkled with wisdom, and his chiseled chin lent a sharp cut to his face, making him highly appealing to women. He was aware of his charms. He rolled the sleeves of his shirt up over his lean, muscular arms, then changed his mind and rolled the sleeves down again. Better to look as proper as possible on the first day of meeting his new birds. Finally, he combed his thick black hair and styled it with a smooth layer of gel to keep it in place. Before leaving, he held his palms up as if taking in some sort of mystical energy. His face turned red, then he clasped his hands together and bowed. Then he grabbed his things and headed to the hotel to greet the new tour, members.

Blank Slate

Raj reached the hotel and was greeted by Meera at the reception desk. She was just signing off from her duty of eight hours and could not resist putting her arms around her handsome hunk. Raj welcomed the gesture. He had really missed her, and as always on the first day of a new tour, he was a little nervous. Her embrace helped to calm his nerves. Wrapping his arms around her, he slid his palm over the skin between the cleft of her sari and her blouse. They murmured in each other's ears and giggled softly. Finally, they let go, not wanting to be overly inappropriate in public. Tired and exhausted Meera ran her hands through her hair; she updated him about his guests, who were currently enjoying drinks in the lounge. Raj nodded approvingly, took a deep breath and walked briskly to the lounge. He had explained the holiday package via email and had tagged each one of them by their hometown, but today he would be able to put a face to each name. It was finally time to meet them all in person.

Starting tomorrow, when the tour would officially start, he would be playing a dual role of not only showing them around the city but also giving them hope about the challenges that had severed them from the societies they lived in. He paused on the other side of the double glass doors to the hotel bar and watched his new birds from a distance for a few minutes. They were engrossed in conversation. He could see their heads nodding and arms gesturing animatedly. A peal of laughter floated over to where he stood.

He smiled and walked towards them.

"Hello everyone."

The tourists stopped what they were doing and looked up. Raj moved closer and introduced himself, and they replied in turn. After the introductions, Raj beamed and exclaimed, "Look at you all! What a bunch of good-looking people! I'm lucky to have you as my tour group."

Darci blushed while the others stared at their drinks or looked away awkwardly. Raj realized that his guests were very shy and quickly got to the point. "Shall we have dinner now?"

They followed him into the dining room, where the waiter nodded to Raj familiarly as he seated them. Darci and Lennard sat next to Raj on one side of the table. The other three individuals sat facing them. Drinks were served and Raj watched his new birds carefully. He saw that Carl was inspecting the others as he sipped his drink. Darci whispered every now and then into Lennard's ear while Asha wore an elegant smile and nodded politely at the others' conversation and sipped mango juice from her tall glass. The dinner had been pre-ordered by Raj, and the tour members found it quite exotic and delicious. Raj kept up a running commentary, describing each dish as it arrived. Asha, already familiar with the cuisine, just served herself and began to eat, while the others eagerly waited for Raj to finish describing each dish before tasting it. They exclaimed over its texture and flavor. It was a merry meal indeed!

Food and music are two magical factors that help strangers bond. The dining area had both, and very soon the five individuals who had come from all different walks of life and distinct cultures were seen sharing thoughts and amusements over various topics. Ira was the only one who chose to eat quietly, which Raj took note of. Finally, everyone was full. They placed their napkins on the table and leaned back in their chairs. The waiter brought bowls of warm water with a slice of lemon to the table, and Raj explained that those were for cleaning one's hands after the meal. There was a loud, collective "Aahhh!"

from all of the international tourists, with the exception of Ira, who merely raised her eyebrows before gingerly dipping her fingertips in the warm water.

Once dinner was done, Raj updated them about the bus that would be coming by to pick them up after breakfast. Lunch would be eaten on the road and dinner back at the hotel. They were advised to carry sunscreen and umbrellas to help fend off the sun. The tourists expressed their mutual excitement for their excursion the next day and departed for their respective rooms. Raj noticed that Ira was meandering back slowly, with a contemplative expression. He chased after her.

"Hi, Ira," he started gently. "Is everything to your liking so far?"

Ira turned around with a slightly surprised look in her eyes. "Yeah! Dinner was good. Thank you!"

"That's good to hear. So—" but then he was interrupted by a phone call. He smiled and raised his finger to motion for her to wait.

She nodded politely.

Raj took a few steps away from her before answering. "Hi Peter," began Raj in a low voice.

The name that escaped Raj's lips came as a sudden shock to Ira. She ventured closer towards Raj, trying to appear as if she was casually admiring the decor. Raj was busy exchanging some information with the person on the call and did not pay much heed to her actions.

"Sure thing, Pete. Be on time here, and I'll see you at my office with the rest of the group." Raj hung up and walked back towards Ira.

"Who was that?" asked Ira in a loud, agonized voice.

Raj was taken aback by her tone. His eyes widened and after taking a deep breath, he replied in an amiable tone, "Nothing to be concerned about. Just some last-minute tour preparations. We will have a new driver tomorrow, and his name is Pete."

Ira was not satisfied. "I don't believe you one bit!" She ran one of her hands anxiously through her long golden tresses as if doing so would calm her. Her petite frame was shaking and her cheeks were turning red. Her eyes looked as if she was about to cry. She began to pace back and forth in front of Raj, glaring at him.

Raj was perplexed. He asked, "Do you have a problem with my new driver, Ira?"

She met his confused look with fiery eyes. "I don't understand! Why would Pete follow me here! Why is he still ruining my life even though I want to live? I just want him to leave me alone!" Tears trickled down her cheeks. She wiped away her tears and went to sit on one of the couches in the lobby.

Raj followed her and seated himself across her. Raj gently placed his hand on her shoulder and nodded understandingly. "It's going to be alright, I promise. I don't think my new driver Pete has anything to do with the Pete you are referring to since my Pete is a good old friend of mine, and I know him well."

A look of understanding flitted briefly across Ira's face, quickly replaced by meek embarrassment. She paused to compose herself before asking, "So, the Pete you were talking to is just your driver? How long has he been with you?"

"Actually, he is a replacement. The driver, Albert, who picked you up from the airport, had a family emergency to take care of. I requested Pete to take his place," he said with a smile.

"Is he native to India?"

"Absolutely!" he said, looking down at his keys. He hoped that this whole "Pete" situation would not ruin the trip for Ira. *Oh, Albert... why?* Raj sighed.

Ira took a deep breath to further compose herself. "Well then, I guess we will just see about it tomorrow, huh! I apologize for my outburst. I just haven't been myself lately. I hopefully, this trip will help to fix that," she gave him a weak half-smile, before getting up and walking briskly towards the elevator.

Raj got up as if to follow her, but decided against it. It was getting late, he should let her get some rest, and get some for himself as well.

"Well, goodnight then, Ira!" he called out after her. Ira gave a quick wave from inside the elevator as the doors began to close. Then she was gone from sight. Raj shook his head and sighed as he walked towards his car. It seemed like this particular tour member was going to be quite a challenge.

While driving home, he got a call from Meera. He updated her on the new guests and she seemed optimistic about them. She offered some kind encouragement about Ira before saying goodbye. Once he was home, Raj laid out his clothes, read over the next day's itinerary and jumped into bed.

Live While We're Young

Raj headed to his office an hour early just to perfect his plans for the day. The tour was beginning. He wanted to help his tourists focus on reflection and eventually wipe out their grudges, thereby helping them to "live while they are young." Each second was as precious as a diamond, and that principle had made him reach success by the tender age of thirty-two, whereas many of his friends were still struggling to find their life paths. While waiting for the bus to arrive, he filled an enormous cooler with bags of ice and submerged a full array of drinks and water bottles to sustain his tour members throughout the day. Just as he was closing the lid, he heard tires screech and a loud honk. He rushed out of his office and waved in excitement at the mini bus.

Peter parked the eight-passenger mini bus and came down to shake hands with Raj. The passengers smiled and waved from inside the mini bus, except Ira, who was sitting stiffly in her seat, wearing dark glasses and a wide-brimmed hat. Raj greeted his birds and asked them general questions about their night and if they were satisfied with their breakfast. It made him happy to see them nodding jovially. Except, of course, Ira.

"Good morning, Ira," said Raj in a chirpy voice.

"Hey, good morning to you too," replied Ira flatly. "I have a request for you, Raj."

Raj nodded, "Sure, what is it?"

"You see Raj, I cannot stand your driver. First I thought it would just be his name, but unfortunately even his body language reminds me of my Pete… So I would like you to fire him immediately." Ira took off her glasses, revealing dark circles beneath her eyes.

Raj was shocked to see how badly she looked. It was a sharp contrast to the day before. He took a deep breath, "Ira, I am so sorry to hear that this is troubling you and I will do whatever it takes to make this right. However, first, I was wondering if you would like to take on a challenge?"

"A challenge?" she asked, apparently becoming even further irritated. "I am not in the mood for any such thing." And with that, she abruptly stood up and walked towards the front of the mini bus.

"Well, I know you are a Marketing Director. Don't people who work in marketing love challenges?" he coaxed in a gentle voice as if trying to cajole a toddler.

Ira shrugged. "You are right about my job title, but I must politely decline your offer." While she spoke to Raj, she eyed Peter with a stern, sidelong look.

"Hmmm… That's fair enough. But I just want you to know that this challenge will help bring you one step closer to happiness…" as he said that, he stepped out of the mini bus.

Ira followed him down the steps. "So, you are firing him. Correct?" Ira asked.

Raj ignored her and kept walking. The others stared out the mini bus windows with inquisitive expressions, watching their little drama unfold. Ira began to berate him; "I knew I shouldn't have picked up that card from my mail box! Some fanatic sends me this crazy information and then I jump on the next plane like a stupid idiot, in a ridiculous pursuit of euphoria! How naïve of me to think that this whole thing could actually work!" she spat, punching the air angrily.

Raj was at a loss for words. Ira gave him a frustrated look and waited for his reply, but none came. The hot morning sun was already beating down on them, and a bead of sweat rolled down her milky-white forehead. Having nowhere else to go, and needing a break from the heat, she stalked back into the air-conditioned minibus. The other tourists gaped at her, but she refused to acknowledge their curiosity. She simply put her glasses back on, while letting out a loud, "Humph!"

Relieved that she was back on the bus, Raj returned and proceeded to give each of his tourists a welcome packet. Then he placed a yellow marigold garland around each of their necks as a form of traditional Indian welcome. The fresh smell of this flower and its vibrant yellow color always gave Raj and his tourist's good vibes as they commenced upon a new journey. However, two of his tourists seemed immune to the positivity of the yellow flowers. Ira had not recovered from her outburst, and Carl had an odd look on his face as well as if there was something he wanted to ask. Raj looked at Carl. "What's on your mind, Carl?"

Carl cleared his throat before asking, "So, is it time yet for us to tell you what brought us here and then you help us solve our problems? 'Cause honestly I am not really interested in this historical tour or dealing with this crazy heat! I am here on an agenda." He paused and continued, "I want my life back!"

Raj was listening keenly to him and put his hand on his shoulder. "I understand, Carl. We all have a vision for how our lives should turn out, but unfortunately, none of us seem to get exactly what we desire, huh?" He scratched his ear and continued, "Unfortunately, solving your problems will not be as straightforward as you just made it sound. You will have to go on the tour with us to get a handle on your life since you will receive valuable insights from this expedition. One by one, your answers will be slowly revealed, as you take part in our historical tour and the other activities I have planned." Raj concluded, trying to make meaningful eye contact with Carl, "Trust me on this one."

Carl was not appeased. He muttered some swear words under his breath, but he remained in his seat. Ignoring Carl's abuse, Raj looked at Ira with a smile. "How are you feeling now, Ira?"

"Carl is a freak," she shot a nasty glare at her fellow tourist, who glared back in turn. "Did you know that he couldn't keep his first or second wife happy, or his children either? Yet, he blames them all for it! I am pretty sure that he's the problem, not his family!"

Raj remained calm and nodded, "Ira, I think you have your own issues to sort out on this trip. How about you just focus on yourself?"

Carl chuckled under his breath.

Apparently embarrassed by Raj's blunt honesty, Ira changed the subject. "So, about that challenge. What was it again?"

Raj was quick to respond, "The challenge is for you to focus your attention on where it really needs to be, my friend. Ira, you are carrying a lot of emotional baggage within you, and, as a result, you have shut out everyone else out. It is time for you to let go of your baggage, cross over your creek of pity, and finally, regain control of your life."

Ira listened attentively, but then she glanced again at Pete, the new driver. "Yeah, about that. Everywhere I go, everything I do, it all reminds me of Pete. We had so many fond memories together. Now I see him at every turn, and those fond memories cause me so much pain. That is the reason I am begging you to fire Peter."

Raj smiled but refused to address her plea. "Now you are aware of your challenge, Ira. Erase those memories by creating new ones, right here, right now! Will you take this challenge head-on? Or will you run away?"

Ira sighed and nodded, "Okay, but just for today. If I don't see some results by tonight, I'm taking the first flight home tomorrow."

Raj nodded solemnly. "Of course, ma'am. You are free to leave whenever you want. Just give it one good shot, okay? I don't think you will be disappointed." He motioned for Pete to start driving. He turned on his microphone and began his speech with a deep breath.

"Welcome to Agra. This city is famous for monuments, forts, and palaces, thanks to its grand history which dates back to the Mughal-era, most notably the Taj Mahal, Agra Fort and Fatehpur Sikri. All three of them are UNESCO World Heritage Sites. Thus making this city a Golden Triangle tourist must-see. This town is synonymous with the history of India and has enriched the nation with its philosophical contributions.

The visitors nodded in appreciation. Carl was amused by Raj's introduction and loudly interjected, "This guy thinks that these old empty walls are really going to fill us with hope, huh? What a joke, huh guys?"

Nobody else acknowledged or encouraged his rude statement, so Raj chose to ignore it and just continue. "Our first stop is the Taj Mahal." At that announcement, there was a sudden burst of excited applause from his passengers. Not wanting to spoil that excitement, Raj decided to put his monolog on hold. He turned off his microphone and took a seat next to Darci and Lennard.

He greeted them warmly in their native tongue. "Bienvenue!"

The couple was delighted. Darci was quick to ask him, "Comment allez-vous?"

Raj gave her a perplexed look, so Lennard quickly translated, "How are you?"

"Merci-Merci!" replied Raj, playfully revealing the limited extent of his knowledge of their language.

Lennard and Darci laughed out loud. Then Lennard added, "Namaste."

Raj blushed and continued in English, "So, what brings you here, Darci and Lennard?"

Lennard replied, "We were curious to know how love can help build a monument. There is so much to experience here in Agra."

Darci quickly added, "We were also hoping that this could inspire us to believe in our love and stay together." Her face was turned to the window, but her voice trembled slightly as she spoke, and her eyes welled up noticeably. Raj noted that Darci's pain seemed to make Lennard uncomfortable. Feeling a little awkward, Raj pretended not to notice her mood.

"Well, you have come to the right place then, my friends," he forced a smile as he spoke. Before he could continue, Pete slammed on the brakes loudly. Raj flew to his feet to see what the problem was. He muttered, "Not again! Excuse me, I'll be right back!" he told his birds and hopped out of the bus to deal with the traffic on the road. Everyone except Ira got up from their seats to watch the entertainment from inside the bus while Pete tried to answer their queries. A few stray cows had wandered into the road, and drivers and passengers alike were trying to herd the cattle out of range of the vehicles, but the cows were not cooperating. Children and chickens were running around as well, not helping the situation. It was pure chaos and most of the tourists were delighted by this loud and unusual mayhem.

Although she didn't like it, Ira was listening attentively to Peter. She found everything about him intimidating, from the tone of his voice to his facial expressions. She hoped that her dark glasses hid the fact that she couldn't stop staring at him. Even though he was an Indian man, he reminded her of her own Pete in nearly every way. She couldn't believe how two individuals from two entirely different parts of the world could have such similar mannerisms. She sighed, cursing fate silently. Was this a cruel joke being played on her by the universe? Or was this the light at the end of the tunnel? Would this strangely similar man somehow help her to drop her emotional baggage of memories and move on? Only time would tell. She leaned towards the window, looking for Raj. Time was ticking and she wanted the tour to get back underway as soon as possible. Luckily, a jubilant Raj reentered the bus with a smile and declared loudly, "All clear!"

The elated travelers cheered loudly, then quickly returned to their seats. Raj seated himself next to Asha this time, who was patiently watching the view from her window. He noticed that she held a pen in her hand and had already started making notes on a notepad. He peered down at what she had written, but Asha noticed and quickly closed the pad. They both exchanged a smile.

"So, what brings you here, Asha-jee?" he asked, affectionately adding the proper Indian term of respect for one's senior to the end of her name.

"Oh, please don't just judge me by my grey hair, Raj. You will just make me feel even older!" she cried, in mock lament.

Raj chuckled. "Okay fair enough, shall I simply call you Asha, then?" he asked, looking into her deep brown eyes, which surprisingly were content. He felt as if she had no regrets about her life.

Asha smiled back at him, "Yes, that would be wonderful. I see the way you have been keenly observing all of us, trying to pinpoint each of our problems. A true mark of a good guide that is for sure. Tell me, what do you see in my eyes?" she asked inquisitively.

"Oddly, I see neither baggage nor regrets..." he trailed off, his voice laden with curiosity.

"Does there ought to be such a reason for this trip, though, Raj?" she smiled as the posed the question.

Raj was taken aback. "No, no, not at all, Asha. It's just that most of my tour participants are recommended via referral. Many of them have similar problems to each other, and so they recommend my services to those who they feel might need me for the same reasons as they did... Yet I have never had a tour participant like you before. Thus, I am naturally curious as to what brought you here and who recommended you."

"I am sure that you must be! I find it surprising that you cater to foreigners. You are famous around the world, yet not here in your country," she added with surprise, dodging his question.

"Well, there are many learned gurus who can guide our natives; thus I never had the thought of advertising myself around here," he admitted.

"Sure, I agree with that. But, still you deserve your limelight. Perhaps I shall be the one to start advertising your services to other natives."

Raj nodded appreciatively as he stood up. "That is very sweet of you, Asha. But there is no need. When my time shall come, it shall happen." he winked at her and walked towards Carl's seat.

Asha smiled to herself and muttered, "It has already come, my friend. It has already come!" Then she scribbled another note in her notepad.

Raj's attention was already honed in on Carl, so he didn't notice Asha's last comment. Carl was looking out the window with a confused expression when Raj put his hand on his shoulder. "How are you doing, Carl?" he asked in a friendly manner trying to push away his thoughts of Carl's angry outrage earlier.

"Man, oh man! Peter is quite an excellent driver!" he remarked to Raj's surprise.

"Huh? Oh! Yes, he is… what exactly brought that to your mind?" he enquired.

"Do you see the condition of these roads? Gosh! The way this driver of yours is dodging all these motorists, cyclists, and potholes. It is truly a talent! The drivers in my homeland could never handle such a challenge with such ease," he explained.

Raj laughed loudly and agreed. "He is my friend first, and then a driver, Carl. And I agree a damn good driver he is!" Paused and continued to inquire, "So, what brings you here, Carl?"

Carl replied, "Well, Raj, I was referred by my lawyer, Ron. Ron Bushnell, remember him? I am currently floating in a soup of problems. My family doesn't trust me. I don't even know if any of them love me. I have worked so hard for my entire life just to provide them with every comfort imaginable, but yet none of them is satisfied! My first wife divorced me, and now I am separated from my second wife. My son won't visit me or speak to me. Ron told me that you could wipe my problems away. So, now can you tell me how you plan on making me happy?" he addressed Raj in an authoritative tone.

Raj took a deep breath and smiled, "Carl, my friend. Honestly, if I had a magic wand for happiness, I would have already waved it for you. But, I don't have it."

Instead of smiling at his joke, Carl's expression clouded with pain. So Raj aimed for a more truthful, yet positive note. "But, you will definitely see a change in your perspective before you board your flight back home. That is my guarantee. All I ask that you do is to be aware of what comes your way during this trip. Ponder over everything you see and hear. And if you have any questions at all, please don't hesitate to ask me. I am fully at your disposal, sir."

Shake it Off

After a long and tiring bus ride, Peter finally announced, "We have arrived at the Taj Mahal!" as he parked along the banks of the Yamuna River. Asha breathed a sigh of relief and was the first one to get up and stretch. This prompted Peter to step down from the mini bus and open the door for her.

"You are quite a quick one, Asha!" he said jokingly.

"I just need some fresh air," she said, taking another deep breath as she stepped into the heat.

Ira stepped out and peered around, craning her neck. "I don't see the Taj Mahal. Where is it?"

"Well it is close by," explained Raj. "We will have to board an electric bus to go the rest of the way. In order to minimize the effects of pollution on such a valuable landmark, regular gas vehicles are not allowed in the immediate vicinity of the Taj Mahal."

Darci stepped down with an excited expression. "Oh! My gosh! Look at that water!" she exclaimed in delight as she ran towards the river. Lennard stepped down slowly afterwards, his eyes fixed on Darci, who was running towards the water.

He crossed his fingers, and muttered to Raj, "I really hope she doesn't do what I am dreading."

There was a loud splash, and everyone turned towards the river to see what had happened. They couldn't believe their eyes! Asha's jaw dropped, and Ira covered her mouth in dismay. Raj assessed the scene, then quickly dashed back into the bus to grab a bag, and went running towards the riverbank, signaling for Lennard to join him. When he reached the banks, he called out to Darci. To beat the heat, she was skinny dipping in the cold waters. Hearing her name, she answered irritably, "What!" She boldly waded over to the men, seemingly unaware that she was completely naked.

Raj kept his eyes fixed on the ground while taking a towel out of the bag and handing it to Lennard. "Come here!" Lennard barked. Darci reluctantly waded over, her hands on her hips in dismay. Lennard quickly wrapped her in the towel, while pulling her along the shore.

"Sheesh! What are you doing, Lennard?" cried Darci restlessly.

"This is not the place to be doing this," he answered softly.

With eyes still respectfully fixed on the ground, Raj added, "Darci, please get dressed in the mini bus." He picked up her clothes and followed them back to where they had parked.

"But, but…" Darci stuttered in a hurt and confused tone.

The two men did not allow her to complete the sentence. They were just busy dragging her towards the mini bus. So she began to cry.

Hearing the commotion, Carl came out of the mini bus and was shocked to see Darci wet, crying, and wrapped in a beach towel. He raised his eyebrows and shook his head as he walked away from the bus to light a cigar. Lennard dragged Darci into the mini bus and seconds later; she came out clothed, which was a big relief to Raj. Then they were on their way. Raj purchased seven tickets and motioned for them to board the electric bus that was leaving for the tour of the Taj Mahal.

Very soon, the globetrotters were able to catch sight of the magnificent mausoleum, which contained the tombs of the Mughal emperor Shah Jahan, and his third wife, Mumtaz Mahal. The white marble under the sun was glistening with purity. The four tall minarets, one on each corner, framed the tombs of the king and the queen. A mosque and a guest house were laid out on either side of the graves. The burial place faced a garden set out in a unique style with a central walkway surrounded by fountains and trees on either side.

The tourists got down from the bus and were approached by local guides who offered their services eagerly. Raj came down the bus last and showed them his identity card, after which the pesky local guides dispersed. He handed some informative literature to each of his tour members and asked them to follow him. Ira declined his request to embark on the journey, and so Peter was tasked with looking after her until they returned.

"So, do you live around here?" asked Ira.

"No, I live in Delhi," replied Peter. "Sam, Albert's friend who is a local here, was supposed to fill his void. He couldn't make it to work, so Raj requested me to take over."

"So, Raj asked and you came all the way from Delhi?" she inquired with a serious pout.

Peter was amused at her question and clarified, "Well, currently I am between jobs. So, did not mind helping out."

Ira gathered the guts to admit, "You know, you remind me of my good old friend, Pete."

"Seriously?" cried Peter in eager amusement. "Wait, is that a good or bad thing?" he added, with a sudden flash of caution.

Ira smiled at his reaction and replied, "We broke up a long time ago..." Her voice turned solemn, "but he was a good friend."

"Oh! I am sorry to hear that," replied Peter.

"Well, you ought to be!" declared Ira, suddenly looking very irritated.

Peter was confused. "What do you mean?"

"Many of your mannerisms remind me of him. The way you move your hands, the movement of your shoulders when you speak, even your smile."

Peter blushed and replied, "So, does that mean that you were checking me out?"

"Uh! Not exactly." Ira flushed. Peter found himself in seventh heaven after hearing the above, and the broad grin on his face was uncontrollable. Ira shot him a petulant look, but Peter was undeterred.

"Let's go join the rest of the gang," demanded Ira, turning away from him and suddenly seeming very interested in sightseeing.

Peter nodded obediently and they walked inside.

Raj was in the middle of showing the group the main chamber, which housed the final resting place of Mumtaz Mahal and her husband, Shah Jahan. "So, tell us the story that they say makes this monument so beautiful and full of love," prompted a curious Lennard.

"Well, the story begins with the marriage of the Emperor to Mumtaz and the passion that the Queen subsequently exhibited. She insisted on traveling with her king wherever he went, even the battlegrounds. They both were true confidantes and life partners, and each other's shields during any time of distress. When Mumtaz Mahal breathed her last breath, she was on the battlegrounds accompanying her king in one such military campaign," explained Raj with heartfelt emotion. Every time he told the story, it nearly brought tears to his eyes.

"So, their love was not contaminated by anything at all?" inquired Carl in an earnest tone.

Raj was taken aback by the word "contaminated," and thought carefully before answering, "Sure, the emperor had two other wives, but Mumtaz won his heart with her relentless love and admiration. The intimacy, deep affection, and attention that Mumtaz gave to her Majesty swept him off his feet, and he loved her more than his other two wives combined, who merely wore the status, 'married' to him."

Carl nodded apprehensively, raising his eyebrows and placing his hand on his chin as he pondered the subject.

"Their love story continues to be an inspiration to countless individuals who come to embrace their boundless love, hoping to carry it forward in their respective lives. Thus making this mausoleum popular in its history, design and romance," continued Raj passionately.

Darci asked if they would also be visiting the graves.

"That, my friend, needs special permission..." Raj paused for effect, then continued with a jaunty smile as he triumphantly waved a ticket at them. "And we have it!"

This impressed Carl, who mumbled, "Thank God, he's worth something after all."

Asha heard that and sneered at him. Carl ignored her look, pretended not to have seen it.

"Oh! Good, you made it here just on time, Ira and Peter!" exclaimed Raj upon noticing the two. "Let's go downstairs so we can continue to walk around the main chamber at our leisure." He showed his badge to the guard on duty. After examining it thoroughly, the guard gave the nod to another guard who immediately removed the barricade for them to enter. The seven of them descended the stairs and entered the chamber where two graves were, each with ornate engravings around them.

The air was surprisingly cold, due to the marble flooring, and there was a strange aura amidst the coolness that caused the entire group to turn quiet. Raj became quiet as well and let everyone get a feel for the ambience. He took a seat on the floor while the rest moved around, taking it all in. Darci sat near a mausoleum marked as Mumtaz and Lennard sat next to the emperor's tomb. Ira decided to sit down near Raj, with Peter promptly following behind her. Raj gave a gentle smile to Ira, who was widening her eyes at him as if she was trying to tell him something. She tilted her head subtly to the eager Peter behind her, and Raj finally got it. He chuckled softly and waved at Peter, who was now sitting next to Ira, and asked him to come and sit next to him. Peter shook his head no in refusal, like a petulant child. Raj smiled, apparently amused, as he shrugged at Ira as if to say, I can't do anything about it! Ira took a deep breath and shut her eyes while tapping her fingers on the floor.

Asha was sitting on the other side of the room, observing the tourists and the guide with a gentle smile, as she scribbled something on her notepad. Carl paced around restlessly for a while, finally settling in the corner that was adjacent to Asha. He fidgeted with the watch on his left wrist as he solemnly glared at the floor. Raj observed his globetrotters. He was especially curious about Asha, who was always writing something. Then his attention turned to Carl. The old man was clearly deep in thought, looking frail and wounded. Even a loud sneeze from Darci did not cause him to lift his eyelids from the floor. Raj felt an urge to go and sit next to him and try to comfort him, but he resisted since he wanted Carl to have this moment of reflection alone with no interruptions.

Darci and Lennard were deep in thought as well, with mellow smiles on their lips, their eyes were pinned on the tombs beside them. Raj felt as if they were having a conversation within themselves and hoped that good would come out of it. They clearly loved each other very much, but needed to bury the hatchet in order to live a happier life together. He hoped to help them open their channels of communication to achieve this.

Then the guide's thoughts were interrupted by soft humming. He looked around to see Peter trying to woo Ira with his melodious tune. Ira, in turn, was swaying back and forth gently along to the melody. Raj nodded his head in delight and was glad that fate had made it easier for Ira to come out of her shell, and he hadn't even had much to do with it. Just then, Raj's phone vibrated. He was quick to get it since did not want anything to distract his tourists. He signaled to Peter that he would be back as soon as he finished the call.

When he returned, he saw Darci and Lennard sitting together in one corner, holding each other's hands and murmuring softly to each other. He smiled and looked at Carl, who was already getting ready to stand up. "Alright, fellas, shall we go back upstairs?" asked Raj.

"Are we leaving now?" asked Darci, wrapping her arms around herself for warmth. Her body was covered in goose bumps from the cool temperature in the basement. Ira was sitting face to face with Peter, enthralled by every tactic of his. Raj's question lifted the spell, and she nodded, getting up to walk towards the stairs with the assumption that Peter would follow her. When she looked back from the corner of her eye, he was doing so, just like a puppy. She loved it and found herself thrilled over the fact that she was playing a reverse role with a guy of the same name. Her ex-boyfriend, Pete was an introvert and she was the one who used to take actions to get reactions from him. Now, his name was the same, but the roles were reversed. She was delighted and charmed by this young man, who was helping her lift the scars from her heart and mind.

All of the tourists were climbing the stairs, except for Lennard. Raj waited for him patiently as he continued to sit in the same spot, which Darci and him had shared. He was sitting motionless, as if still deep in thought. Raj called his name gently.

Lennard looked up, "Hmmm?" he questioned.

Raj approached him with a concerned expression, "Are you okay?"

"Yeah, I am fine. Just thinking of what actually happened between us, and why I do not have the courage to either let go or accept it," he replied, blinking back tears.

Raj seated himself next to Lennard, "So, what really happened?"

"Well, now that I see the tomb here, it was nothing as substantial as this, but wonder why I still can't let go…" Lennard took a deep breath and closed his eyes. "It happened exactly three years and eight months ago. I got fired from my job, Darci was the only breadwinner in the family, but her salary was not enough. Our mortgage, monthly payments, and other expenses were still the same and one salary couldn't cover it all. The extreme financial crunch was straining our relationship, and amidst all of that, she disappeared for a night." he paused and rubbed his forehead while his eyes became moist.

"I was frantic, calling her cellphone, her friends, her family, and no one could track her down. Finally, I reported her as a missing person to the police. A case was opened, and next morning I heard from law enforcement that she had been found." He took another deep breath before continuing. "I took down the address from them and reached the hospital. She was unconscious. I went near her bed and took her hand. I looked for injuries, but to my dismay, I did not find any. Then a nurse came around and said, 'She can go home now.' I asked with utter confusion what she meant by it. The nurse said, 'The procedure that she had last night looks to have healed. So, when she regains consciousness, she can go home.' She left and I still had no idea what she meant by it, so I did not give up. I followed her, shouting down the corridors of the hospital at her, 'What procedure? What happened?'

She refused to answer me, and I was lost. I rushed back to my wife, who had regained consciousness and was sipping some apple juice. Seeing me, she smiled and hugged me. I was equally elated to see her well, so hugged her back tightly. I squeezed her so tightly that she asked me what was wrong. I asked her what procedure she had had the previous night. She sat on the bed, touched her belly and spoke with a pensive tone, 'Lennard, I am not mad at you over anything. I had to make a significant choice since money has been so tight over the past few months.'

'What is going on? What is all this about?' I snapped at her.

Darci took a long breath and continued with moist eyes, 'Lennard, I had an abortion. I was pregnant with your baby, but considering our current financial situation, and our constant arguments over it, I did not have the heart to tell you something that would involve more expenses.' Ever since then, there has been this awful silence between us. I have been avoiding talking to her even though she has attempted to raise this topic many times, but I just can't face it." Lennard looked at Raj with damp eyes.

Raj put his hand on his shoulder and patted it sympathetically. "I am so sorry to hear about this." Lennard nodded appreciatively, acknowledging Raj's support. Raj got up, and Lennard followed too. "So, Lennard, what do you plan to do about this?" asked Raj with curiosity.

Lennard was taken aback by that question, and asked him back, "What do you mean, Raj? Do you even know what it means to lose someone so close to your heart?" he posed in a raised voice, frowning.

42

Raj paused for a bit as if an arrow had pierced his heart. He gulped and muttered softly, "Yes... kinda..."

Lennard was too preoccupied to notice it and began climbing up the stairs. Seeing that Raj wasn't following behind him, Lennard shouted out, "Are you coming, Raj?" Raj slowly trailed after Lennard, still dazed.

The other tourists were hanging around the upstairs chamber. Asha was wandering around with Carl, to Raj's shock. Ira and Darci were hanging out with Peter, who was clicking pictures of them in different poses, as the ladies giggled and whispered amongst themselves. Raj was happy to see a smile on Ira's lips. Then he looked at Lennard and urged, "You know, by not facing your fear, you will waste this life of yours. It is high time you figure out what you really want. I also made a similarly difficult choice in my own life." he paused and then added firmly, "It's been three entire years, for god's sake. Do not waste your life over a mistake that was done as a favor. Look at her, she is still sticking around." Then Raj walked away without waiting for a reply. Raj's encouraging words transfixed Lennard, as he admired Darci from a distance.

"Hi fellas," Raj greeted Carl and Asha enthusiastically. Carl turned around with a smile on his face, which Raj found very unusual. Asha was also in an equally elated mood; thus, the guide came to the point. "What are you two smiling about?" he demanded playfully.

Asha was quick to jump in, "Well for a change, I am appalled by the behavior of your guest here, Raj." She pointed at Carl, who blushed and waved his hand as if trying to say, *Let it go.* Asha continued, "He brushed aside a couple of goons who were actually getting fresh with me! Even though I requested him to leave this matter to me since I could tackle those bunch of youngsters, he insisted on getting rid of them. And his adamancy to help has actually impressed me." Asha smiled appreciatively at Carl.

"Carl, thank you, my friend," Raj said while extending his hand towards him.

"Oh! No need for thanks! This is the least I could do for a friend in our group," Carl gushed with enthusiasm.

Raj thought to himself, *This is the first time I have seen a cordial side of Carl! Whatever he was thinking down there, is doing wonders. Jai ho!* Raj allowed himself a satisfied smile.

Then the guide announced, "Let us tour the outside of the minarets and the garden. We will form two groups. One group will come with me, and the other will go with Peter. But all of us must promise to stick with our assigned group until we meet at the bus stop in an hour's time. We are on a tight schedule and can't afford for anyone to wander off and get lost. Does that sound reasonable?"

Everyone agreed. Asha, Carl, and Lennard chose to go with Raj, while the girls were happy to stay with Peter. Peter and his group broke off, and he dutifully followed the girls, taking pictures every so often, when demanded. Ira was so enthralled by Peter's attention that she carefully chose the cutest poses to get him to look at her. Darci noticed it and teased her. Ira did not care to disclose her hidden agenda to Darci so she just smiled at her teasing and laughed along. While throwing her arms up in a particularly cute but precarious pose, she slipped on the shiny marble floor, hitting the ground with a loud thud. "Ouch!" she howled in distress.

Everyone around them suddenly stopped and stared at her with piercing eyes. Ira was not used to the nosy concerns of passing old ladies, who were being addressed as "Aunties" by Peter as he tried to answer their multitude of queries. The first aid kit that Peter always kept buckled around his waist came in handy, and Darci quickly helped to patch Ira up. "Gosh, those old ladies should mind their own business!" Ira scoffed. Darci echoed her statement while Peter disagreed for once.

"They were just concerned about you, Ira. They mean no harm," he said with a straight face.

Ira was stunned by his response. The insecure Ira crept in, and she thought to herself, *Is this the end of the honeymoon? Are the tables going to be turned and I will be pursuing him from now on, just like old times?*

"But that's not important. What matters is whether you're okay," added a concerned Peter, leaning down and placing his hand on her shoulder. Her old Peter's mere touch had caused a thump in her heart and a swarm of butterflies in her stomach that would make her blush. She bit her lip and then smiled. But this Peter's touch had no such reaction. This gave her tears in her eyes because she did not want their flirtation to end so fast. She pulled Peter by his shirt towards her lips.

Darci went, "Awww…"

Peter was stunned; his eyes wide open as she grabbed him. But he did not wait even a few seconds before giving in to what she wanted. They kissed passionately until quite a few heads began to turn and look towards them. Peter realized, and let go of Ira. Adjusting his shirt, he looked around and smiled and waved at people awkwardly.

Ira was also wearing a happy face. Their kisses had caused the butterflies that she'd been hoping for.

The three toured the garden with Ira holding Peter's hand and Darci tagging along, at times feeling out of place. But she had no choice since Lennard was still in denial. While looking at the dome of the Taj Mahal, she prayed and hoped that she and Lennard would be in love forever until death took them apart. Darci was extremely tempted to put her feet in the fountain water. She called out to the couple that was walking ahead. Peter agreed to wait for her since he had this feeling that Darci and Water just might be synonyms for she just couldn't resist herself dipping in it. "As long as you are fully clothed. I don't mind waiting for you!" he joked with a wink.

Stunned by what Peter just said, Ira slapped him playfully in the stomach, while Darci smiled. Ira and Peter watched from a distance while Darci enjoyed seeing her reflection in the clear water as she waddled her feet in it, enjoying the sprinkles that splashed across her skin. She closed her eyes with a happy smile, savoring the feel of the cold water on her feet. She giggled so loudly that some passersby even began to stop and stare.

Suddenly an unexpected voice broke through her happy moment. "Do you have a minute to talk?"

Her eyes opened wide. She could not believe what she just heard. "Talk? Yes, Lennard, I have been waiting for this for a long time!" she exclaimed, as she got up and made eye contact with him.

Lennard felt uncomfortable as Darci looked deep into his eyes. He blushed and suggested that they walk along the garden as they talk. Darci was quick to comply. She waved at Peter, who was engrossed in Ira. She signaled to him that she would be with Lennard, and would meet them at the bus stop.

Peter nodded, happy to have uninterrupted time with Ira.

Darci wrapped herself around Lennard's arm as they walked. She realized how stiff he had gotten, and slowly pulled her hand away from him. She cleared her throat. "So, what do you want to talk about?"

"About the incident that occurred, three years and eight months ago."

Darci went red hearing that he knew the exact length of the episode, "Boy! Has it been so long that we have not gotten intimate, and yet I still yearn for you?" she remarked loudly, completely uninhibited.

Lennard stopped immediately, turned towards Darci, and pinned his lips gently on hers. Darci's eyes shut as she melted, her legs giving way as if they couldn't support her any longer. Lennard was quick to hold her. They stayed in that position for what felt like a very long time. Then finally Lennard let go, but Darci insisted on hugging him, pulling him tightly towards her chest. Her petite frame reached Lennard's chin as he fondly rested his jaw on her head, inhaling the scent of grapefruit, gardenia, amber and mini busilla in her recently-shampooed hair, and reminiscing about those old days when they would stay in this position for hours, just talking and cuddling.

Darci finally broke loose and looked Lennard in the eyes, "Seriously though, is there anything you want to say? I have apologized so many times and stayed with you despite your silence." she said sincerely.

"I'm sorry…" Lennard uttered softly, and continued, "but the fact that you chose to abort our child without my consent makes me feel uncomfortable and has haunted me all of this time."

"I understand, but you could have talked to me about it sooner.

The fact that you chose to be silent has just made things worse." Ira grumbled. "Now, what's next?" she demanded, putting her hands on her hips.

Lennard sighed, feeling nostalgic. "Remember the times when we were dating in school? I was always considered a nutcase for sticking to my guns over issues that were contested for days! That's just how I am!" he looked at Darci pleadingly.

"A nutcase?" she reiterated with a severe frown. "I think you are more than that. Do you realize how much time we have wasted over just this one incident? We could have had two more children in that time. Now that we are financially stable again, we could have tried to conceive a second and even a third time." She paced back and forth, attempting to control her frustration. "I know you are a tall man, but..." she hesitated. "You have a small shadow. You go into your shell when something hurts you since you don't have the courage to face it. You need to speak up next time that something bothers you. If this happens again, I'm leaving you."

Lennard was hurt by her words, and nodded quietly, as they walked towards the bus stop. Darci took one last hopeful glimpse at the dome behind them, wishing that she could reconcile with her lover and have a romantic ending to their story.

Soon everyone was seated in the mini bus. As Raj surveyed his tourists, he could sense that many had matured in just the past few hours. The stress lines that had caused them to travel overseas were no longer as dark and distinct. He turned towards the Taj Mahal and gave it a small salute of gratitude. Then he instructed Peter to drive to the day's lunch restaurant, where they were pleasantly greeted and served palatial platters of food.

The tourists ate with additional pleasure because their hearts were deliberately lighter. Watching the reactions of his guests over the lunch table, Raj marveled at how much more appealing food could be if the heart's needs have been attended to. He remembered how little Ira had eaten when she arrived in India, in comparison to how heartily she was digging in now that she had the admiration of a new Peter. That fickle heart, taking command of the rest of the body's needs and wants! Amused by this odd organ, he patted his chest in appreciation as he reached for another spoonful of curry. Once the bowls of water and lemon came out, signaling the end of the meal, Raj announced that he would be taking the guests to their hotel for a nap, because, after tea, they would be heading out to the Taj once more, to see the mausoleum under the full moon.

"That is an excellent idea," said Asha, as she wiped her hands with the napkin. The blazing August sun had taken a toll on her and her head was pounding. Agra had a well-deserved reputation for being one of the hottest tourist destinations in India. The humidity was appalling and could leave even a native puffing for some coolness as the daytime temperatures hover around 113-118 degrees Fahrenheit if there was no rainfall. Unfortunately, it was one of the days, when it was dry and the heat and humidity were taking a toll on everyone.

The others agreed and hurried towards the mini bus, eagerly anticipating jumping into their clean sheets after an afternoon of exciting but tiring emotional breakthroughs. Quite a few rigid thoughts had melted and there was a lot for many of them to think about. Once the mini bus parked at the hotel, they were instructed to meet again in the lobby at six. They lumbered off to their respective rooms, needing to digest their food, as well as attend to the swirl of emotions within themselves.

Raj went to the lobby and waved at Meera, who was still on duty. Seeing him from a distance, she requested a five-minute break and ran to meet him. They stepped out of the lobby and Raj was relieved to see her calm, serene face after that intense rush of emotions he had witnessed in his traveler's faces. He held her hands and kissed them, and they exchanged a few small words and jokes, interspersed with light kisses. Five minutes flew by quickly, and she reluctantly headed back behind her desk. Raj reentered the hotel as well, to discuss the menu with the chef for that night's dinner.

Darci filled her tub with water, looking forward to a pleasant soak while Lennard crashed onto his bed. Soon a soft humming filled the air, indicating that Mrs. Jensen was enjoying her time in the bathtub. Just then, a sudden knock interrupted her bliss. She grew quiet when Lennard asked her to hurry up in an impatient voice since he needed to use the restroom. She didn't answer at first, but after another hard knock on the door, Darci grumbled and got up. She threw a bathrobe on and opened the door, looking wet and annoyed. "You knew the door was open, you could have just come in without interrupting me!" she spat. As per usual, Lennard ignored her, rushing in to do his business. He left wordlessly, plunking himself back down onto the hotel bed. Darci had a dark expression on her face. She hadn't been expecting things to return to the status quo so quickly, not after the heartfelt words and passionate kiss they had shared earlier.

After drying off, she went to sit next to Lennard on the mattress and bluntly confronted him about his behavior. She asked why he had been so romantic before and was now back to being so cold again. A tear threatened to drop from one of her eyes, but she held it back. Yet despite her passionate plea, all that he said was, "Love was in the air!"

Speechless and stunned, Darci got up without a word. She walked over to the other queen size bed and she plopped her body down, letting out a couple of mournful sniffs. Peeking out from under the damp strands of hair that hid her expression, she saw that his nose was already buried in a book, like always. Humph! She was suddenly glad that they had chosen to ask for a room with two beds. Since they had a total lack of intimacy ever since that fateful incident, sharing a bed just wasn't necessary. In fact, they both felt much more comfortable in a space of their own.

Meanwhile, Asha wrapped her wet head in a towel as she flung herself onto her bed with a rueful expression. Her feet hurt from walking and there was no one there to care for her. Whenever she was as exhausted, or sad, it made her miss Abhay even more. When he was alive, he was the best kind of company when she was physically or mentally exhausted. How he would nurse her like a baby and make her feel special! As Asha reminisced those days, she felt fresh tears trickle down her cheeks. She was quick to wipe them away and reached out into her purse for a couple of sedatives, quickly popping them with the glass of water on her nightstand. She was a strong woman and she had to carry on, no matter how difficult.

That was Asha's mindset ever since her husband passed away. It was nearly fifteen years ago. At that point, she had to pick herself up, dust herself off and learn to carry on. She had two sons with Abhay and was proud of the fact that she had sent them both to high school and had helped them through graduation. She was proud that she could do it in spite of her parents' constant pressure to remarry. They had been so sure that she would not be able to care for her children without a man in her life, but Asha believed otherwise. Her resolution had paid off, and she had proven to her beloved, and now dearly departed, parents that she was able to do it all by herself. With Abhay gone and her sons successfully settled abroad, her nest was empty and all she needed was a companion. So she had hired a full-time maid from a reliable company. Kamala was always helpful when she was in need of a massage, a warm meal, a helping hand, or merely some support or advice.

"Oh Kamala, how I wish you were here!" she groaned as she covered her eyes with a scarf and rolled around to catch a snooze.

Finally alone in his room, Carl took a satisfied breath as he poured himself a drink, pondering over the lines in his palm. He had always considered himself a rational man, not one for superstition and old wives tales, but he couldn't resist a bit of curiosity after watching a palmist sitting along the path at the Taj Mahal. He took a pensive sip of his Scotch, relishing the sharp, aged taste, and hoping that he too, had matured for the better over the years.

In another room, far down the hall, Ira turned on the shower, peeling off her sweaty clothes. She stole a glance at her thin frame in the bathroom mirror, and couldn't resist a small smile. She still had what it took to attract a man! Her budding romance with the new Pete in her life was proof, and she saw herself with new eyes. Her smile widened, and she winked at the cute girl in the mirror. Her self worth had plummeted ever since the old Pete had left, and her body had withered along with her confidence. Things were finally starting to take a turn for the better, and she couldn't be more relieved. She hopped into the refreshing shower, letting all her cares from her old life rinse away. She was filled with high determination to make new memories and erase the old. Then she hit the sack, falling into a profound and restful sleep.

The Long and Winding Road

The clock struck five o'clock as Raj arrived at the hotel cafe. Carl was the first to join him. He looked rather tipsy. He was using the chair as support, to keep his balance, and swayed back and forth, struggling to place himself correctly into the seat next to Raj. Raj was shocked to see him in that state since the sun had not even set yet. He got up to assist the older man, and could not resist saying, "Gosh! Carl, you seem quite drunk!"

Carl had to blink twice to process what Raj said and appeared to find it very offensive. "No, my good sir, I most definitely am not!" he retorted, while continuing to sway dangerously back and forth. Raj was starting to fear that Carl might accidentally break something.

The words that came out of Raj's mouth next surprised even him, "Well, I am sure this is nothing new, 'cause you have always been drunk with power!" He inhaled sharply after speaking the insult, already dreading his guest's reaction.

"Power! Oh yes! I love power, Raj," Carl agreed while seating himself opposite Raj "Do you have any objections to it?"

"I have no problems with it, my friend," Raj answered. "It is you who needs to watch out, since that feeling of power may be suppressing the parts of your brain that govern inhibition, and the result is right in front of you."

"What do you mean?" Carl asked, peering at Raj in confusion.

Raj ignored him, beckoning to the waiter.

"Coffee or Tea Sir?" asked the server.

"Both please, and some snacks as well," answered Raj.

Soon, their table was filled with cookies and tea sandwiches. Carl helped himself to the spread and took deep gulps of black coffee.

Raj was relieved to see Ira arrive. Carl had been quite the handful so far and he was grateful for the new company. Ira seated herself on the other side of Raj with an unexpected smile, pleasantly greeting both men. Raj smiled back and offered her tea while Carl continued to stuff his face. Next, Asha approached them. Raj was pleased and intrigued to notice that Asha's arrival brought a smile to Carl's face.

"Oh! Raj, my headache is still appalling…" Asha groaned as she seated herself next to Carl.

"Did you take a painkiller?" asked Raj with sympathy.

"I did, but I guess the heat has taken quite a toll on me. Please do remind me to bring a scarf along tomorrow," said Asha with a sigh. She was so used to asking for reminders from Kamala that she put the request forward without a second thought.

"Have some tea. You will feel better, I promise," suggested Raj as he beckoned the waiter to bring another pot of tea for the two women.

Asha looked around, and upon noticing Carl in his drunken state was puzzled, "What happened to you?" she asked with curiosity while placing her hand gently on his arm.

"Asha, your country is mixing me up in a soup of emotions! I have never felt so slippery before!" he mumbled in a drunken attempt to explain himself.

Asha's eyes widened, and she asked him to explain further, while Raj listened intently, amused.

"You see," began Carl, "all of my life I have worked on my own terms, but now I find myself feeling completely and utterly out of control! I suppose that could mean I may have a turnaround in some sort of positive way... but it is making me feel so confused! I want to want something that I gave up on long time back..." he managed, taking another gulp of his black coffee.

Asha gazed at him with wide eyes, apparently still puzzled.

"I want Barbara back!" cried Carl. "I want my kid to come back and live with me. My business needs him, and it is the time that I retire. I want to spend the rest of my days with her," he added with moist eyes, which gradually gave way to a gush of tears.

Upon sight of those tears, the table turned awkwardly silent. Ira, Raj, and Asha were stunned by his confession and stared at him. Feeling a little guilty, Raj extended his hand towards his guest and crooned, "How can I help you?"

Carl took no time at all to respond, "You know Raj, I saw this palm reader sitting by the side of the road near the Taj Mahal. Could you take me to him?" he pleaded.

Raj was taken aback. He exchanged a glance with Asha and pondered the best answer carefully.

Sensing Raj's hesitation, Carl added, "Actually, if it is too much of a hassle, I can go by myself in a taxi tomorrow!"

"That's not the problem, Carl," Raj began. "The problem is that we do not know how valid this palm reader may be, and that makes me wonder whether you should trust him."

"Well, I saw that many people getting up with a happy face once their palms were read by that gentleman!" Carl noted.

Asha decided to cut in, "Carl, sure they may have had a happy face once they left him. But the question is whether their wishes will indeed come true."

"What do you mean? If it is in my destiny, I will get it. If Barbara and Marx are in my fate, I will reunite with them! Or else, why should I spend my remaining years longing for them. Then I might as well hunt for a new love..." his eyes wandered in Asha's direction as his voice trailed off.

Asha made a sour face, and put her cup down, ready to clarify a few things for him, but Raj was quick to cut her off. "I would not mind taking you there tomorrow, Carl. But please remember that you ought not to make your destiny based on such decisions. To do so would not be doing justice to yourself and your life. And you are quite an educated man to be relying on that kind of superstition."

Just then, Darci and Lennard arrived. They looked refreshed after their nap; however no one could sense that things took a U-turn in their relationship after Lennard bounced back to his old self. All of the conversation was dropped, and the group set about to demolishing the last of the snacks and beverages. Once the plates were empty, and all of the teapots and carafes as well, they were ready to embark.

Raj walked out to the driveway to find Peter with the mini bus. They went over the evening's plan while the tourists seated themselves. Once everyone was settled comfortably, Peter looked towards Raj for a signal to start driving. He was amused to see that Raj was just staring at the entrance of the hotel as if waiting for somebody. Peter had a feeling he knew who Raj was waiting for, and sure enough, a dainty female figure soon came running up to the mini bus. Raj greeted her with a broad smile and introduced her to the others.

Everybody was happy to see her. They were acquainted with her since she had greeted each one of them at the front desk upon their arrival and had attended to their daytime calls. Meera was equally delighted to be there with all of them. She had just gotten off work for the day and had changed into her casual clothes. Raj had been quick to remind her in the morning to pack something to wear for the evening's journey. Since the Taj Mahal was always romantic no matter how many times one visited it, she had chosen a particularly lovely outfit for the occasion. Her hair was braided, she wore a delicate pastel skirt and blouse that matched the colour of her skin. She was looking forward to admiring the Taj Mahal under the full moon light.

This kind of scenario had its own charm and was every lover's delight. Raj always made sure to have her beside him when he was on any such excursion, and she was equally elated to give him company. Their relationship had lasted over two years, but neither was in a hurry to make a permanent commitment. They were quietly enjoying their time together, and taking things slow. They had met via a common friend at a party and were keen to focus on their careers. Since there were no strings attached, both found each other's company provided the best of both worlds. They were each other's shoulder to lean on when one needed support, each other's entertainment when one wanted to share laughter, and each other's pleasure when their appetite for lust arose.

Meera took the window seat in the front row and Raj took the aisle seat, beckoning to Peter to start driving. He hoped that there wouldn't be any more traffic obstacles and they would reach their destination without incident. It was another trip to the Taj Mahal, but this time the weather was cool and humid with a high chance of rain. The air conditioner was off, and the windows were open. The fresh breeze made Ira's hair flutter, and she pulled it to one side of her head as she gazed out the window, watching the street life of the city in reverence. She couldn't believe how the locals all seemed to have such broad and genuine smiles, despite the poverty they lived in. Back home, people were so stressed out, and got so easily upset over even the slightest thing, whether it was their coffee shop running out of their favorite flavor, or their personal driver getting stuck in traffic. People in Agra didn't seem to have such silly worries.

Fortunately, the evening traffic was much better than what they had faced earlier in the day, and before they knew it, Peter was parking near the Taj Mahal again. Raj kept his eye vigilantly focused on Darci, hoping not to have to deal with a repeat of the embarrassing skinny dip incident. Since he was a frequent visitor to the Taj Mahal, he wanted to keep his reputation respectable to avoid being mocked by the other tour chaperones, who were quite a gossipy bunch. He paused, frowning over his thoughts and wondering what a "respectable reputation" really meant anyways, since trying to live based on what other people think is insane. All people have different perspectives and there is simply no way to please them all. To even attempt to do so would be maddening. He sighed. At the end of the day, as long as he knows he has made a difference in someone's life, why should he care what others think? He nodded to himself, satisfied with his conclusion. He ushered his guests out of the mini bus and onto the electric bus to the mausoleum, where they entered the main chamber.

The moon was shining bright yellow, like a loyal companion overlooking all the creatures of Earth. The same moon that silently floated over the fields, the calm lakes, and the rooftops of darkened houses. The tourists looked up, comforted by the sight of it hanging gracefully above them as they ogled at the beauty of the Taj Mahal. Every full moon night has a different story to narrate, and that evening, it told the story of this handful of hopeful but weary travelers, all with pains in their heart that they were ready to lay to rest. Raj reached for Meera's hand, softly squeezing it as he contemplated the full moon that shone above them, listening to the story it told. Sometimes the adventure is weak and wan, but tonight it felt like it was reciting an epic that was high and full of light, as if it was trying to tell him what it meant to be a human being. Doubtful, cryptic, and imperfect, yet sometimes humanity could rise to create something as beautiful and lasting as the Taj Mahal.

The tourists were filled with reverent silence, and the only sound heard that evening was the clicking of cameras as mankind assembled there. Tourists and guides alike were mesmerized by the beauty of the monument as the full moon beamed above it, bringing to light the essence of the glowing white marble. The majestic monument was equally authentic and classic as it highlighted the spirit of love. The shadows cast on the Taj Mahal moved slowly as the planet and the moon shifted their positions simultaneously, almost as if waltzing to a soft music of their own making. This breathtaking scene mystified many pairs of lovers that night, as they clasped each other's hands and promised to remain by each other's sides. Raj and Meera were one of those romantic couples, and Meera was glad she had dressed for the occasion. Looking into Meera's eyes, Raj was filled with love and devotion that was unmatched by anything he had ever felt for any other woman. However, not all of his tourists were having such feelings. Many of them still had to wrestle with their demons before opening their hearts to their significant others like Raj and Meera had.

After making their way throughout the Taj Mahal, Raj's tour group lingered in the garden, where they marveled at the architecture and the engravings that were lit up by the moonlight. They might have stayed there forever if it wasn't for the call of the electric bus driver, interrupting their thoughts. They were the last group to board the electric bus, and they made it to their mini bus just in the nick of time! As soon as they were seated in the coach and Peter had closed the doors, a heavy downpour began to fall upon the metal room, followed by lightning, and loud thunder. Their nostrils were filled with the fresh smell of wet mud, and their minds were collectively transported into a moment where they each experienced a vivid picture of their favorite memory, no matter how different each person's life was. They were all too absorbed in their thoughts to notice that they all wore small, contented smiles and had goose bumps on their arms due to the sudden chill from the rainstorm. Then the magical moment passed, and their dreams were interrupted by the sound of locals in the street outside the bus, running haphazardly in search of shelter. Asha smiled as she watched the commotion, recalling her youth. She had had her share of adventures and remembered running through the streets in the rain when she was a teenager, caught in some storm or another while shopping at the market or having tea with her schoolmates. Those were the days. They used to laugh and jump over puddles, even though they were drenched, eventually coming home soaked to her worried mother, who would bundle her up and serve her soup or hot tea. As one grew up, the rain became more of a nuisance than a time to have fun. But as a grown woman, Asha could also appreciate the gifts that such rainfall would bestow. She smiled knowing that the farmers would be grateful for a good harvest thanks to the torrential rains.

As they circled the perimeter of the Taj Mahal, where vendors displayed their wares, Carl kept a vigilant face pressed to the window.

He was determined to find the spot where the palm reader had sat so that he could point it out to Raj when they came back the next day. He noticed that some of the passers-by who walked beneath the vendors' awnings were occasionally putting their heads out to get some sprinkles on their faces, and this act seemed to fill them with an incredible look of joy. This observation made Carl curious, and he wanted to try it too. He opened his window, and put his head out, facing upwards and laughing loudly. Then he ducked back into the shelter of the bus with a satisfied expression.

Darci noticed his behavior and followed suit. She shrieked with excitement, which naturally upset Lennard. He was about to yank her back into her seat when he overheard Meera and Ira, who were seated behind them. Meera was about to stick her own head out into the rain and was encouraging Ira to do the same, but Ira didn't seem to be very interested in doing so. Her past was once again giving her nightmares, although she had been trying to get rid of it, her skin was crawling and she found herself yearning again for her old Pete. Her heart was filled with self-pity and her eyes were filled with tears, but nothing could change Meera's mind. She adamantly opened the window and pushed her head out, crushing Ira on the way, since she was seated between Meera and the window. Meera's chuckling made Ira curious. When Meera pulled her wet head back inside, Ira met her eyes with a perplexed expression. "Wow, this is so refreshing!" Meera exclaimed. "You really must try it!" Ira didn't reply but slammed the window shut.

Darci nodded in agreement with Meera's words, wiping her face with her bare arms. Her love for spaghetti strap tops suddenly seemed like a bad idea. She was soaked, and wouldn't have minded a more substantial layer over her exposed skin.

Ira eyed Meera and Darci carefully. At first she was jealous hearing their happy sounds, but then after a brief pause, she began to wonder if she would be filled with the same joy if she could only try it... Her curiosity eventually forced her to reopen the window, and after a minute's final hesitation, she gingerly placed her head out, turning her face up towards the dark sky, which was filled with violent crackles and booming thunder. The water drops on her cheeks made her close her eyes, and her body lurched forward as the cold wave swept inside of her. It was as if it was quenching a deeper thirst, perhaps the agony of those darn memories that she couldn't get rid of. Time seemed to stop for her; she was in such a state of pure exhilaration. Her head was out for so long that her seatmate felt the need to gently tap her thigh, checking to see if she was okay. Ira opened her eyes and was quick to pull herself inside. Meera was pleased to see that Ira's smile was refreshed and bewitching. She seemed as if she had just woken up from a deep sleep.

"I loved it!" Ira exclaimed in delight, as she wiped her face on her corduroy jacket. Some of the droplets had trickled down her neck and into her V-neck dress, tickling her breastbone. She laughed softly, dabbing herself with the fabric.

"You look so… fresh, Ira!" remarked an enthusiastic Meera.

"Yeah, I know!" replied Ira jubilantly. She continued, "I feel so different and alive. Now just if I can just continue being like this all the time," she crossed her fingers, "I can possibly iron out that crease within me and change up my life."

Raj noticed all the excitement and wondered if Asha was too old for that kind of stuff. So he asked her if she would like to join in the fun since she was quietly staring out her window. Asha promptly declined his offer, adding, "You know, I am too old to get myself wet! Who will nurse my ailing joints?"

Raj nodded sympathetically and smiled.

Asha brushed her hair aside and bent forward, pointing at her knees, "I have to see to my health because rains tend to lock my joints. When these intersections are left wet, they become worse."

Visibility was at a minimum, but Peter was up for the challenge though slightly disturbed over an episode that happened at the mausoleum. He eyed Ira from his rear view mirror. Her golden hair was blocking her face, but he could see her deep in conversation with Meera. He could not make out the expression on her face; she appeared to be in good spirits. Seeing that made his heart sink. His head was filled with questions, and he struggled to make sense of them as the incident came flashing back to him. He already had a lot of feelings for Ira and had wanted to take advantage of the romantic view of the Taj Mahal, hoping that it could help him take their flirtation a step further. He had tried to hold her hand while they were gazing at the beauty of the monument, but she had refused to grasp it. In fact, she even moved a few inches further away from him. *I thought she liked me, so what is going on? What should I do now? Does she fancy me or not?* Peter lamented to himself, trying his best to stay focused on the perilous road.

"Are you okay, Peter?" inquired Raj, noticing the mournful expression on his driver's face.

"Yes, of course, Raj. Is there a problem?" replied an irritated Peter, pushing the gas pedal a little harder than normal.

The sudden acceleration caused Raj's heart to skip a beat and he decided not to press the issue since the weather outside was not their best friend. He smiled and waved back at him, shaking his head. He leaned forward and lowered the background music to lessen any distraction it might cause for Peter.

Peter didn't reply but merely frowned deeper, as he tried to figure out where to drive amidst the deepening pools of water that had accumulated along the road, due to the inadequate local drainage systems. The way could hardly be seen, and it was difficult to make out whether any vehicles lay ahead of them either. Peter was relying on his judgment and experience. Horns blared from every car as if trying to alert the other drivers of their existence. Traffic was slow since all the drivers were in the same state of confusion.

Peter was getting annoyed by the slow traffic and was trying to overtake a slower car with a constant blow of his horn, but the driver refused to budge. This irritated him further since he couldn't stop thinking about what had happened with Ira. She had been checking him out for quite some time and preferred his company while sightseeing, so then why wouldn't she hold hands with him and acknowledge their compassion when the time was right? Those thoughts filled him with agony. He continued to honk at the driver ahead of him and when the driver refused to give way, he overtook him from the right, slammed on his brakes, pulled down his window, and when he was adjacent to the car, cursed the driver loudly. Then he accelerated the vehicle, which jolted everyone in the bus since they had not seen this side of Peter yet.

Ira was especially taken aback by his attitude and wondered if she had anything to do with his sour mood. She realized that lately she had been thinking only about herself and her own happiness. She was aware that her companionship with Peter was a bit of a rebound relationship, since she was so eager to erase her old memories, and hoped that a new man could help wash her feelings for the old Pete away. Unfortunately, it was becoming apparent to her that her feelings for the old Pete were as stubborn as her tears, and now she feared that both would never cease.

Sensing the growing chaos, Meera got up and sat next to Raj. They reached for each other's hands, and Meera placed her head on Raj's shoulder. She whispered something in his ear and nodded fondly. Ira watched them from her seat, and their evident warmth made her realize how cold her behavior at the mausoleum might have seemed to Peter. Filled with sharp remorse, she tried to get up to apologize to him, but the bus was going too fast, taking sharp turns at an unsafe speed. Her legs gave way, and she fell backward into her seat.

Raj glanced at her and called out, "Do you need something, Ira?"

Ira blushed and shook her head no.

Peter was too busy navigating the wet roads to notice. He was caught up in his thoughts and the bad weather, as he juggled the steering wheel, trying to keep the bus under control. His arm muscles were growing sore and stiff, and he could feel a tension headache building within his skull to which he tried to occasionally rub his head while taking deep breaths, but it wasn't helping much. He was fighting mixed feelings of aggression towards Ira and his circumstances. He cursed Sam, who could not take this assignment thus, fate made him meet these tourists especially Ira. A feeling of apathy overtook him as he continued to honk loudly and swear at each vehicle that he passed on the road.

Carl was amused by Peter's bad behavior. He couldn't resist jeering, "Boy! I thought I was good at cursing. You beat me there, buddy!" Carl clapped his hands in admiration.

Raj was not amused. He got up from his seat and carefully maneuvered towards the driver, holding on the railings as he swayed down the aisle. He patted his hand gently on Peter's shoulder. "Are you okay? Do you want me to take over?" he offered.

Hearing Raj's kind concern, a sudden feeling of guilt flowed into Peter, who immediately apologized for his behavior, but insisted that he was okay to drive. Raj was quick to excuse his behavior and sat back down next to Carl, keeping a watchful eye on his driver. Raj smiled at Carl, "Tomorrow we plan to visit the Agra Fort after our brunch. If you still want to visit…" he paused, unsure if Carl wanted the others to hear about his desire to have his fortune told.

Carl quickly replied, "Sure, I would still like to visit the palmist. I did not see him in the evening, so I hope he will be around during the day."

"Yeah, those people typically leave by sunset. He should be around tomorrow." Raj replied. "So, make a list of the questions you want to ask him. It will be easier for you to get a reliable conclusion that way," he advised.

Carl agreed with his thoughts.

Suddenly, Peter felt scorching and flushed. He opened his window, and, of course, a deluge of water came violently splashing in. The spray hit some of the passengers as well, and Carl was quick to swear loudly.

Asha could not take Carl's cross behavior anymore. She tapped his shoulder, "You *do* realize you are the oldest in this group, don't you, Carl? Show some class." she asserted.

Carl nudged her hand away like a petulant child and averted her gaze.

Peter's hot flash was followed by a sudden feeling of cold, and he quickly shut the window again. He had a confused expression on his face, and he was peering out the side window as if trying to remember something.

Raj noticed his odd behavior and asked, "Is something wrong?"

"Where are we going?" inquired his driver.

Hearing that comment, Asha and Carl shared a knowing look. Asha shuddered, afraid of what might come next. Carl reached for Asha's shoulder, squeezing it comfortingly.

Before anybody else could comment, Raj flew out of his seat and grabbed the steering wheel. "I'll take it from here. Please go have a seat, Peter," Raj commanded.

Peter, frowned, giving the guide a confused look, "Is there a problem? Am I not doing my job well?"

His eyes were locked with Raj, and his foot was pressed firmly on the accelerator pedal. Irritated, Raj gripped the wheel tighter and tried to pull Peter up from his seat, which made the driver push his foot further down onto the accelerator. Meanwhile, the storm outside was growing worse. The sky was tar-black and filled with large clouds. The sound of the pounding rain and vicious lightning was akin to the buzzing of angry bees.

Then the women on the bus shrieked loudly. Peter and Raj had lost control and the bus veered violently off of the road, flipping upside down, and sliding through the mud. There was an awful thud as the front of the bus collided with a tree. The hood crumpled, and the trunk came crashing through the front window, barely missing Raj. The horn was blaring, glass was cracking in all of the windows, and then there was a fiery explosion. The heavy rain quickly wiped the worst of the flames out, but tiny ripples of fire continued to smolder in the remaining puddles of gas. Finally, there was a cacophony of grinding and popping as the wheels and hubcaps scattered themselves across the road.

All of that noise was followed by complete silence as the traffic around the crash screeched to a halt. Passerby shouted for help, and some people came running towards the accident. Smoke was still rising from the front portion of the vehicle when the paramedics arrived. The storm had slowed the arrival of medical help, and nearly an hour had passed since the crash. When the paramedics shouted into the bus, looking for survivors, they could only hear their own echo. They knew that no survivor was going to be able to walk away from this accident. They made plans to drag out whatever unconscious bodies they could find and hoped for the best.

First, they noticed a semi-conscious body lying just outside the perimeter of the bus. Deciding that he must have been a passerby who got hurt in the accident, they put him on a stretcher and sent him to the hospital. Then, they began the search for survivors. Since the front and back windshields had both been broken, along with the windows, those holes were a good access point for the EMT's, who took precautionary measures to avoid cutting themselves on the shards of broken glass. The first EMT to enter the bus took a deep breath as he climbed slowly through the broken back window, hoping that life was still in there, but there were blood marks all over the handrails and seats. He took a moment to shut his eyes and take a deep breath to focus on his goal. Then he moved forward, checking the bus row by row. Soon, he found seven unconscious bodies. The passengers were lying either face down or face up with most of their faces covered by their hands or arms as if to protect themselves from the catastrophe. How amazing is a man that he tends to use the upper limb of his body when in danger or excitement, thus making them very essential parts of the frame! The EMT checked each limp wrist, feeling for their pulses. Breathing a relieved sigh after registering seven shallow but steady heartbeats, he paged his colleagues, who came rolling in with stretchers. They loaded all of the victims into ambulances and sent them to the nearest hospital.

Before leaving the scene, the paramedics reported the accident to the police. They said that they had recovered seven individuals from the bus, and one passerby who had been hurt as well. Nobody else was found in or around the accident. The ambulances had been sent to Life Line Hospital. The police investigated the bus, looked for any way to contact the family or friends of the injured. Since eyewitnesses had said that foreigners were evacuated from the bus, the police were extra concerned about solving the case, since they did not want this incident to reach their respective embassies and turn into a scandal. All they were able to find on the bus was a few miscellaneous items; a makeup bag, a sun hat, some water bottles and snacks, and a binder with "Raj Touristry" printed on it. There was an address and telephone number imprinted with the name. They quickly called the tour company, but since it was a one-man travel agency, the phone went unanswered. That led to a dead end.

The hospital's ER was buzzing with sirens as nurses and attendants hurried in and out with stretchers, until all the seven individuals from the bus were in respective rooms and were being attended by doctors and nurses who tried to bandage their broken bones, stop their blood loss, or give them respite from severe pain by injecting pain killers. Their names were unknown so they were identified based on their physical characteristics.

"The blonde girl is regaining consciousness, Doctor!" shouted a nurse. The doctor came rushing in and began to ask her questions about who she was while the nurse checked her vitals. "Ira..." mumbled the girl softly, and then cried out due to the pain. Her name was noted and she was given an analgesic that made her fall into dreamland.

"The old Indian lady is moving her head from side to side, Doctor!" declared another assistant as she bandaged Asha's head. "What is your name, Madam?" asked the nurse.

"Kamala... Kamala..." murmured the old woman with pain. The name was noted.

In a nearby room, Lennard slowly regained consciousness as well, and after giving them his personal details, he agreed to take a sedative to help himself go back to sleep and heal. Meera and Carl awoke soon after, both following the same pattern as Lennard.

However, as the others snoozed peacefully, two individuals still had not regained consciousness. They were transported to the Intensive Care Unit (ICU) while Ira, Meera, Carl, Lennard and "Kamala" were moved into one big room in the hope that seeing each other's faces as they drifted in and out of consciousness would give them the hope they needed for a speedy recovery.

Meanwhile, Raj was in another hospital since he had been identified as a bystander who was at the wrong place, wrong time. He had bandages on his face, arms, and legs. He wanted to talk, but since he was so heavily drugged his speech was slurred, and the nurse could not make any sense of it. She left him to rest, marking his name as "Unknown" on his chart.

Wide Awake

The nurses and doctors were getting tired. They had been making their rounds trying to help as many patients as they could and that included those seven individuals that were wheeled into the emergency ward about eight hours earlier. Doctor Batra, the head of the department, had been assigned the cases of the seven patients from the accident since it involved foreigners. The police were still trying to track down the origin of the individuals and their treatment needed to be top notch. As the doctor took notes on their progress, he became confused about the setback suffered by one male and female patient and was pondering over a solution. Just then the nurse walked in, "Doctor! Len is awake and wants to see you."

Doctor Batra checked his log, and corrected her, "You mean Lennard?" he inquired.

"Yes, Lennard." she corrected herself.

He got up and walked towards the large area of the ward that held his special patients. There was a curtain in between each of their beds to give them privacy when needed. Lennard was forcing his eyes open. The potent analgesic tended to put him into a deep sleep and upon seeing the doctor; he waved at him sleepily.

"Hello, Lennard. I am Dr. Batra. But, you could call me Dr. B," he extended his hand towards him.

"Oh! Good!" Lennard replied. "I don't see my wife in this ward. Where is she?" he inquired, fearing for the worst.

"Are you talking about the lady with short brown curly hair?" the doctor asked.

"Yes, yes. Have you seen her? Where is she?" Lennard smiled, eager for more information. He wriggled upwards into a seated position, supporting himself on the bed rails.

"She is still unconscious," replied the doctor with a grim face. "But we are working on her, and her vitals are gradually improving, so in no time she should be wheeled back in here with you."

Lennard wanted to see her.

"But, you are not in good enough shape to be doing so…" cautioned the doctor.

Lennard refused to comply, banging his fist on the bed in anger. Doctor Batra was quick to signal for a wheelchair. Once Lennard was sitting in it, he rolled him to the ICU, where his better half was wired to various gadgets. Seeing that sight, Lennard grew, even more, emotional. The doctor patted Lennard's shoulder comfortingly, assuring him that his wife would recover soon.

"You have to make her well, Doc. She is my life," pleaded Lennard, brushing away his tears. "I cannot imagine my life without her…" he said, putting his hand on Darci's. He gently caressed her fingers, especially the one with her wedding ring. Seeing his beloved laying unconscious in front of him, filled Lennard's mind and body with catastrophic havoc, and he felt as if he was on the verge of a meltdown.

Dr. B made some notes about Darci, jotting down some critical points with respect to her health after getting a brief overview from her husband. Lennard looked exhausted, and the doctor suggested that he rest. After promising her that he would return, Lennard agreed to be wheeled into his ward.

Meanwhile, the police tracked down their mini bus information via the department of motor vehicles and got the names of the driver and the owner. They tried again to contact Raj, but there was no response.

This was because the owner of Raj Touristry was lying on a cot in a different local hospital. Despite being bandaged and heavily dosed, he would periodically shout the names of the seven other individuals from the bus over and over. His attending nurses and physicians just gave him blank looks and smiled while cajoling him and insisting that he would be okay. Thinking that he was crazy, they didn't even bother looking up the names that he was shouting or asking him any further questions to clarify the situation.

Raj wanted answers and since they all were clueless, he was getting impatient, and increasingly vindictive to any health officials approaching him. This drove Raj crazy, but he could not do much except wait. So he shut his eyes to sleep and heal.

Two days later, all of the patients were still in the hospital. Ira was getting a grasp over her aches and pains. Her twisted leg was getting put in a brace to speed up her recovery. Looking around, she noticed that the people on the beds around hers looked very familiar. There was a strange emptiness inside of her that haunted her, and she wondered why. She had this odd urge, an adamant desire to do something… to say something… but she couldn't quite remember exactly what it was. The high-intensity drugs that were being continuously injected into her made her thoughts dull and sluggish.

Then she suddenly heard a chuckle that made her feel liberated. She felt a sudden longing to laugh as well as if the emotion had belonged to her once upon a time. Her desire was unyielding, and her mind started to connect the dots until she eventually thought of Peter. She looked around the room but did not find him. Her heart pounded, and she took a big gulp. She called out to the nurse who was attending an old Indian lady for her sprained knee.

"What happened, Ira? Are you in pain?" asked the nurse with apprehension.

"I need to know about Peter!" she exclaimed.

The nurse looked around the room, paused, then inquired in a gentle tone, "Are you referring to an Indian male with a tall frame and a medium complexion?" she asked inquisitively.

"Yes! That was exactly who I am referring to. Where is he?" she asked as she tried to get up from her bed. The nurse helped her up and informed her that he was in the ICU.

Ira was panic-stricken, and she pleaded the nurse to take her to him. The attendant paged the doctor for permission, then she was wheeled into the Intensive Care Unit, where Peter was laying unconscious. He was hooked up to an oxygen tank and had bandages on one of his arms, his head, and his neck. Ira shrieked, then quickly covered her mouth with both of her hands, not wanting to disturb him. Tears trickled down her cheeks, and she did not restrain them from flowing. She looked at Peter's face, covered in bruises and beckoned the nurse to bring her closer to him. As Ira was wheeled towards him, she looked at his lips, thinking of when he would hum such beautiful notes that she would burst into laughter, while throwing her head back, and allowing her hair to fall all over her face. She thought of how he used to brush her hair out of her face, giving her goose bumps. She wrapped her arms around herself, in order to pacify the skin erections that had erupted due to the memories, but just then she gave out a soft screech as her right shoulder was in a brace, and it was painfully jolted by her sudden movement. The doctor asked if she was okay. She nodded, continuing to look at Peter. She wondered how a person could crave for happiness even if it were only for a few hours. While staring at Peter, she murmured a quiet thank you and put her hand over his, gently stroking it.

"I really want you to get better, Peter. You know, I was making new memories with your presence, and erasing out the old," she murmured in his ear. The machines next to Peter suddenly beeped, prompting the doctor to check his pulse.

He reported with a happy smile, "Whatever you are saying seems to be helping him. Keep it up!"

Ira brightened upon hearing that and eagerly continued to whisper sweet words and jokes to Peter. The doctor left them alone, assuring her that he would be back in a few minutes. Ira smiled and reminisced on all of the good times they had shared during their short time together. Then the nurse came in, and declared, "Time's up!" Wheeled a drained but happy Ira back into her bed. After Ira had rested for a couple of hours, the doctor approached her in the hope of getting more information about Peter. He was happy that he had tracked down the driver, but he still wondered where the owner was.

On the other side of the town, Raj was getting stronger. Once he could speak properly again, he managed to address his doctor as Raj, the owner of Raj Touristry. That was enough to create a buzz in the hospital. The bus accident had been all over the news. The police had hit a dead end with regards to their investigation and had reached out to the news media to help them find the tour company's owner. Once Raj's identity was known, things started moving at a lightening pace. Very soon, law enforcement rushed to the hospital to meet Raj. After a few brief questions, he was transported to the same hospital where his tourists, driver, and girlfriend were being treated.

He felt as if he was being reunited with his family and was wearing a broad smile when he was wheeled into the shared ward. His bed was set up next to Carl's, and while the doctor checked his vitals; he was updated on Darci and Peter, who were still in the ICU.

"Peter is showing small signs of recovery now and then, thanks to Ira. But Darci has been in a coma with a low pulse ever since she arrived at the hospital." the doctor informed Raj.

"Does Lennard know about this, Dr. Batra?" inquired Raj.

"Yes, he does, and, unfortunately, that has set back his own recovery, since he has wanted to go and sit near Darci's bedside most of the time. The additional stress is wearing on him considerably," he lamented.

Raj was speechless at first. Then he thought about the mysterious ways that fate and love often worked. Strange misfortunes sometimes lead to an unexpected silver lining. He looked at Doctor Batra, speaking with a newfound assurance, "I have hope that something good will come out of all of this, Doctor." Doctor Batra seemed a bit puzzled, but nodded politely and smiled before leaving the ward to check on other patients.

After the doctor had left, Raj sat on his bed, waiting patiently for his roommates to wake up. Carl was the first person to greet him.

Carl sat up in his bed and his bandaged leg twisted, causing him to swear loudly.

Raj shook his head from side to side and murmured, "Some things never change. How are you doing, Carl?"

"What are *you* doing here?" replied the old man loudly "In fact, what are we all doing here? Thanks to you and Peter, huh! I had never imagined that my 'life-changing' dream vacation would lead me to a hospital bed. I don't want to die like this..." he paused since his eyes had gotten moist, and continued solemnly, "Not just yet." Then his tone changed. "You know, I could sue you for this!" he narrowed his eyes.

Raj was amused by the emotional rollercoaster Carl was riding. "Sure, Carl. I don't mind. In fact, I am planning to reimburse all of my tourists for the money they have spent on this trip. Of course, that will leave me close to bankrupt..." he sighed and turned away, wiping a sudden tear from the corner of his eye. The thought of hitting rock bottom financially filled him with sadness and fear. His future was uncertain and bleak. He pushed the unpleasant doubts from his mind and continued. He was emboldened by the thought of Meera's smile, and the many other happy tourists who he had guided in the past few years. "But I am sure that if I keep working hard, I will eventually earn it back. I have faith in the positive testimonials I receive from tourists like you, and I am sure I have done a good job so far," he finished with a smile.

"Oh yeah! You deserve it, Raj," Carl rolled his eyes sarcastically. "I am actually gonna sack my lawyer for recommending me to you! My problems were bad enough as it was, and now I have just had a near-death experience in a foreign country. Look at my hands! My cuticles have so much dirt in them! Eww, I can't even eat food with these hands!" He shrugged his shoulders in disgust. "Yesterday evening, I actually requested that the nurse feed me!" Carl pouted and looked away.

Raj could not control his giggle.

"What is so funny?" Carl snarled.

Raj cut to the chase. "Carl, do you want to speak to Barbara?"

Carl whipped around to face Raj again, looking both tempted and irritated.

"You know, at this stage, if you called her, it could be a win-win situation for you." Raj proposed. Carl did not understand Raj's point and stared at him with confusion. Raj continued to explain. "You will get sympathy and concern from her since you are injured, and it will also help you to heal faster when you hear her voice." He winked at Carl, "What do you say, old man?"

"So, you mean to say that we will Skype? That way, she can see my condition and the state I am in?" he said, with a pathetic expression.

"Sure, we could do that, Carl. What do you say?"

"Oh! I am in!" he said enthusiastically with a wink while pointing his finger at him in jubilation. But then after seeing his dirty claws, he scowled, and stuffed them under the sheets.

Dr. Batra made the arrangements by contacting Carl's separated wife for a request to Skype and made sure that she was online. Once the phone beeped, and the confirmation was made, an amused Carl was wheeled out to the doctor's office to use his Internet connection. Raj was happy to see Carl was stepping out of his comfort zone and hoped that it would be a success. Carl was emotionally and physically at rock bottom, so chances that he would allow his ego to come in between him and Barbara was close to zero; however, Raj kept his fingers crossed and looked around the room in hopes of finding Meera in one of those beds.

Just then, the nurse entered to give medicine to the old Indian lady. The nurse was calling out, "Kamala, Kamala," softly, but the old woman was not responding. The nurse swore, plopped the medicine down next to her bed, and was about to walk out of the room, when Raj signaled to the nurse and gave her the correct name. The nurse was surprised to hear that they had been calling Asha by the wrong name all along. She woke her up gently, using the correct name this time, and gave her medicine. She inquired about the name mix-up, and Asha, who had just ingested her medicines, was in a better mood. She realized what had happened and laughed while explaining to the nurse about her home companion who had looked after her for the past five years. Anytime she had an ailment, she chanted her name. That made the nurse give out a hearty laugh and she left the ward still giggling as if she could not wait to tell her friends.

"Raj, happy to see you. Where were you?" inquired Asha, once she was able to sit up on her bed.

Raj gave her the full saga of where he had been, and how he got here while Asha listened attentively. "You know Asha, you had wanted everybody to know about my job, and this accident made headlines in the paper! We even were given a two-minute segment on national television!" he joked, then turned serious, telling her that he hoped that Darci and Peter would soon come out of danger.

Asha looked down, fidgeting with her sheets. His words reminded her of the journal that she had lost in the accident. She had been making notes about the trip so far, but now she had to rely on her memories alone. She wondered if her brain was still able to register all that had happened. She saw her knee wrapped in gauze and chuckled. Memories are definitely made when a mark is left on one's body, thus making this trip a memorable one!

Lennard had just been wheeled in. He had just been in the ICU talking to Darci, who still showed no sign of improvement. Seeing Raj, sitting on a bed, he first rubbed his eyes and then requested the nurse to wheel him next to his bed.

"Raj! Raj" he shouted out.

The nurse went, "Shhh…. there are some patients who are sleeping, please not so loudly, Sir!"

Lennard did not care, and he was not to be blamed. Sometimes when man's plate is full of emotions, whether he be happy or sad, he tends to get overwhelmed by it, and that actually forms a bubble around him. This bubble does not allow anything to penetrate inside him since his mind is already excited from the happiness or devastated by the catastrophe. Unfortunately, Lennard was sailing in a boatload of desolation. His wheelchair halted near Raj's bed, and he wanted to tell him everything about Darci.

Raj lent a sympathetic ear with vigilant eyes as Lennard delivered the news. Asha was also listening, and even the number of years she had lived so far, could not help her speak any comforting words of wisdom.

"Raj is that you? " came a weak voice from one of the beds that had curtains drawn. Raj immediately recognized the voice, and while putting a hand on Lennard's shoulder to show empathy for his grief he replied, "Yes, it is. How are you Meera?" he inquired with compassion.

"Oh my god! Where did you go? How are you?" she cried out loud, trying to get up. But the plaster casts she wore kept her bedridden. She rang the bell, and the nurse took a while to come. The waiting period was mortifying for both lovers. Meera could not help but comment out loud, "Damn these curtains!" Finally, the nurse arrived, and upon her request, the curtains were pulled away. Meera felt it was a grand finale event as her left hand went over her hair and bruised face, more so to assure herself that these things were in order and she was looking presentable enough to face her sweetheart.

Presentation has always been the key for any individual. Is it the lust between two lovers that makes them look at their respective reflections prior to a meeting or just the fact that appearance is the key and it helps to start conversation between two known or unknown people?

Raj saw her hand and leg in plaster and wanted to go and hug her, but his own leg was bandaged and he would have needed assistance. Besides Lennard was weeping next to his bed, and Raj did not want to be insensitive. They exchanged looks that were deep and profound and after scanning each other, they felt better.

In the meantime, Ira was wheeled from the ICU and was in a happy mood. She got even more excited upon seeing Raj and shouted out to him. "Peter has blinked his eyes and is showing signs of improvement!" She was filled with even more happiness after seeing the group's curtains open and all of the other patients sitting up. A smile stretched across the faces of everyone present except Lennard, who grew, even more, dejected, and slammed his fist on the arm of his chair. That action was noticed by Raj, and he took a big and a silent gulp, as he hoped for things to improve for his friend. Lennard was undergoing emotional turmoil, and needed to let go of incidents that did not favor him. He understood that circumstances can lead to an unfavorable turn of events, but his inability to get over the past was creating problems in many aspects of his personality and life. He was unable to properly verbalize his feelings and thoughts, which was making things even harder for Darci. And now, she was not even able to pick up his hopeful vibes since she was in a coma.

Just then Carl was wheeled in, looking as happy as a puppy at a dog park. He had spoken with Barbara and had even shown her his dirty claws. She had been very sympathetic and had urged him to come home soon so that she could help him through his recovery. She had even agreed that when they met they could discuss their future.

Raj shook hands in delight with his tourist friend. To him, Carl was more than just a tourist, just as he was more than just a guide to Carl. During the trip, all of the tourists opened their emotional cans of worms to their guide, thanks to the testimonials from their friends who had done the same, and managed to get good advice and come to find a solution. Thanks to Raj's backing and counseling, they found the clarification and meaning they were missing in their lives.

It is amazing how sharing of one's intimate details can make human beings forget the formality of a relationship and bring them closer together. They can identify themselves just as mere humans since we all share the same kinds of mental states. Emotions tend to entwine Earthlings together. Happiness and Sorrow are the two fundamental states that we all go through, and when shared with another person, we benefit from invaluable support and guidance. Humans are fascinated by emotional material. We are always intrigued by the news and tragic events that are covered in the TV, radio, and newspapers. But our attention spans are often brief because soon we get involved again in our own problems.

Raj, however, was not a typical person. He was a different breed who preferred to listen attentively and show genuine interest in the problems of others, instead of focusing only on his own. He thrived on being around other people, getting to know them, and accepting them for who they were instead of judging them. He was a guide who was appreciated by many because he chose to share their emotions and life experiences. That trait is actually the hallmark of any good friend or lover. This benefits both parties by leading to a greater sense of connection and closeness.

Carl had moist eyes as he stared into Raj's eyes, "Was this mishap pre-planned?" he asked jokingly, but he was also filled with a strange curiosity.

Raj smiled widely while patting his friend's arm with affection. "That scar on your shoulder will remind you to stay grounded while in the company of your wife, once united with her. She might just reconcile with you if you can maintain this humble attitude." the guide said with confidence.

"Gosh, I have to keep reminding myself about it then! It's gonna be tough, but I will try." Carl paused and continued with a shine in his eyes, "Maybe we could visit you again as a couple, and that might help celebrate and renew our life together!"

Raj nodded encouragingly.

By then, it was getting late, and nurses began helping Carl and Ira settle into their beds while attending to their needs. The doctor came in to check the vitals of all his patients before he retired for the day and was happy to see their progress had improved significantly. Being a sensitive person, Peter was showing signs of recovery thanks to Ira's care. His pulse was stronger and his vitals were showing progress. The doctor had to just wait until he opened his eyes. But Darci was still being held back by something, and it was delaying her from regaining possession of her body.

Lennard chose to park his wheelchair next to Raj's bed. This made Raj request a chair for himself so that he could spend some private moments in conversation with him.

Dinner was brought into the ward. The combination of oil with spices did not give out as appealing aroma as the hotel's food would have. But that's what makes the difference between hospital and hotel food. When food is cooked with the spices and sauces that make it delicious and give it a distinctive smell it often loses its nutritional value. Therefore, a meal that is prepared to heal a body is blanched and boiled without much flavoring to preserve the nutrients.

"Should I feed you Carl?" asked a nurse, as she helped him sit up.

"Nah! I am fine now!" replied this tourist to her surprise

The nurse then brought him a warm bowl of water and lemon so that he could cleanse his hands before eating. The bowl filled with grayish dirt from under his nails and he grimaced sheepishly as he handed it to her. Just as she was about to leave with the bowl of dirty water, he muttered a soft "Thank you." Then he paused and continued, "You know, you have helped me heal in many ways. Your short grey hair even reminds me of my wife. Actually, we are separated at this moment… no, *divorced,* but I had the guts to communicate with her today anyways, thanks to my friend Raj." Carl looked into the nurse's eyes appreciatively.

She nodded with joy. Nurse D'Souza was an older woman in her sixties who had been a nurse for nearly thirty years. She had seen many patients come and go and had always been regarded as just an attendant to nurse their wounds, look after their personal hygiene, a mode of transport when pushing a wheelchair, or a helper to attend to drips and other medical devices. Rarely did they ever confide such personal words in her, or thank her so warmly for her services. Carl's words of gratitude gave her goose bumps. Those thankful words were usually reserved for only the doctors. She blushed as she placed the plate of food on the portable table that was placed over his legs. Her eyes were low and she felt quiet and self-conscious. She put the bottle of distilled water on the table adjacent to his bed, and adjusted the ringer next to the bed, asking him to ring it, if any need arose, then she walked off to get him a new change of sheets.

It is amazing how one expression of gratitude can make a person melt and go beyond one's capacity to do something for another individual. This magical feeling was mutual since Carl was undergoing a strange lift in his spirits. He was currently less self-centered and more relaxed after speaking to Barbara. This had triggered happy memories within him, which were making him act more social and kind than usual. Nurse D'Souza's dark under eye circles seemed a little bit lighter. Whatever the cause, but she smiled optimistically at her patient, telling him that he would be out of his casts in no time. Carl felt a unique connection with her, and that caused a surge of self-satisfaction and happiness within him. Asha was quietly observing the scene and felt happy about Carl's emotional progress, which could eventually lead him to have a physically fit self as well. She nodded at Carl and gave him a big thumbs-up. Carl accepted it with grace and returned the gesture.

Meera's bed was next to Ira, and while they ate their dinner, Ira went on and on about Peter. Meera was listening attentively at first, but eventually she grew bored. In hopes to make Ira shut up, she interjected rudely, "So, do you love Peter?"

Ira was dumbstruck. She paused for a long time and pondered the question while pushing her spoon around her bland bowl of curry. She snapped irritably, "First of all, that is none of your business!" Then she took a deep breath and calmed down, "I have told Peter that I am making new memories in order to overwrite my old ones. So, whether I love him or not has not really come up between us. I don't even know if that is important right now. I am just focusing on improving myself." Then Ira put the spoonful of curry into her mouth and met Meera's eyes defiantly.

Meera was not happy with Ira's response. "Peter is a sensitive guy, and I don't really know the whole story about what caused this accident, but you ought to behave like a grown woman and give it to him straight."

"But I love it when he tries to butter me up!" said Ira, defensively.

"Sure, you enjoy it. But you better either start reciprocating or tell him to cool off. Because you are toying with his emotions! If you are not interested in something serious with him, then don't lead him on just for your own amusement!" cried Meera. "Tell him what your intentions are, Ira. 'Cause if you don't change, you will leave India with happy new memories, but he will be left devastated," she added sternly.

Her words were a harsh blow to Ira's heart. She nodded, and continued to eat her tasteless food. "Thanks, Meera," she replied cordially. "I did not think of it that way until now."

Meera smiled back. "You are welcome. I am sorry if I was hard on you. I just want the best for you and for Peter. He is a great guy."

"No, it's okay. I am glad you brought it up since I have been thinking a lot about myself lately," replied Ira in an equally remorseful tone. "The last thing I want is for Peter to go around trying to erase his memories of me by finding someone who looks like me or has a name that rhymes with Ira!" she added with laughter.

Meera found that amusing and jumped on the wagon, "Oh! Gosh, that would be terrible!" she said with a wink, "Imagine him looking for someone with a name like Indira since that would be the closest rhyme available in India." They both laughed as they finished their dinner trays. A smile and an apology at the end of any argument serves as a balm and giving pure relief from all the harsh words that took place. Such simple tactics, and yet not many know when and how to use it.

Raj and Lennard were wheeled by the attendants into a covered area of the patio. Then they asked to be left alone. One of the attendants handed them a buzzer to press once they wanted to be transported back to their ward. The city was under the spell of rain, and the trees and plants in the garden were swaying to the tunes of Mother Nature. Left and right went their movements, as if dancing to the tune of some music playing in the background, and the smell of the wet mud made Raj take deep breaths. The hospital ward had been giving off a sterilized odor, and he was grateful for fresh, fragrant air. He allowed soft sprinkles of rain to fall on his face as he twisted his head towards the sky. The smell of nature is exhilarating since it arouses the sense organs to absorb the maximum, which actually uplifts the spirits of a man and it helps him to heal himself on a physical and emotional level. Raj was enjoying that process even though he was accompanied by Lennard, who was growing ever more impatient. Sometimes a man needs to put himself first, since healing oneself makes one able to better serve others. Inner strength is essential to be able to aid others. If one has enough inner strength, then he can truly be a pillar of support that gives others their wings to fly.

"So, tell me Lennard, what encourages you to wake up each morning?" asked Raj, while wiping water drops from his forehead.

"My alarm clock, of course," replied Lennard with a frown, implying to Raj that he thought it was a silly question.

Raj had to pause upon hearing that answer. He continued, "Ah! That's stupid, huh? It definitely has to be an alarm clock. How else would man wake up to do his chores?" with a smile trying to fit in with his traveler's mood.

Lennard smirked and shrugged his shoulders to show his approval.

Raj changed his approach, asking, "Lennard, how do you plan on tackling the mistakes you made in the past?"

Lennard was very honest about it, "When you do something wrong, it stays in the present, no matter how much time passes."

Raj was shocked by his statement, but then realized the impact of the situation today between him and Darci. He could not resist saying, "No wonder Darci is still in a coma."

"Excuse me?" interjected Lennard.

Raj did not bother to apologize, coming to the point with a rather stern voice, "Lennard you ought to forget your past and learn to laugh a little. You know, whatever happens, happens for a reason, and it is all part of a divine plan unfolding from the level of the soul."

This left Lennard feeling utterly confused, and he rubbed his chin while looking inquisitively at his guide.

Raj could see his confusion, and blinked a couple of times before uttering any more words. Unfortunately, Raj was not speaking his language and that was leaving both of them dry and cold (metaphorically speaking) even though the atmosphere was moist and humid. Raj tried again to get his point across, saying only, "Just let it go!"

"Huh?"

"Freedom is letting go, Lennard." Raj asserted, and continued in a mellow tone, "If you let go of what isn't real in your life, what's left will be real. Darci is real, that baby is not." Sometimes, a physical touch makes another person realize the impact of the words. Raj had exactly that in mind as he placed his hand on Lennard's shoulder.

This time, Lennard nodded understandingly. Raj breathed a deep sigh of relief, and continued with some words of wisdom in order to push the antidote deep within Lennard, "Now that you are aware of your feelings, take note of your emotions. Try to use reason and be objective, while detaching yourself from the energy that binds you to your past, which actually drains an individual."

"It's gonna be difficult, man!" Lennard shrugged his shoulders and rubbed his temples.

"Yes, it will be difficult, and your body will ache since you have metabolized your past and given it sanctuary in your body. Do not restrain your body. Let it tremble with fear and convulse with anger when your memories come back to haunt you. However, be aware that you must not inflict this negative energy onto Darci or anyone else," Raj cautioned.

"Phew, sounds tough! But I will try my best to be aware of my energy from now on!" sighed Lennard.

"Good, Lennard. Just remember that the past is a false guide to the future, and yet it is what most of us depend upon. You must look forward and remain positive. The present is the time period that counts." Raj said with a smile.

Lennard took some long deep breaths and watched the raindrops falling on the ground. He carefully observed how the rings of ripples grew and extended around where each drop fell, eventually skimming across the surface of the water. Somehow, the rain resonated within him and gave him new hope. Raj realized that Lennard needed some time alone, and beckoned for an assistant to wheel him back to the ward.

Take Care

After a few silent moments, Lennard rang his bell. "I need to see Darci," he urged the attending, nurse.

She looked at her watch, "But—"

He interjected, "No buts!" then toned down his voice, "Please!"

The nurse felt his pain, nodded apprehensively and wheeled him into the ICU.

Darci was laying still. Since she was breathing insufficiently, the ventilator was on and it made loud noises as the machine maintained the flow of air into and out of her lungs.

Lennard was at her bedside, and as he touched her fingers, memories started to gush into his mind. His emotions flickered across his face as he experienced a multitude of flashbacks about his relationship with Darci. His frown would be overtaken over by a slight smile, and vice versa. The nurse noticed his expressions and realized that he needed time alone, and politely excused herself. Lennard played with Darci's fingertips and drifted off to a time when the couple would entertain their guests with their dual craftsmanship at the piano. He remembered how their fingers swept through the notes over songs such as, "Pirates of the Caribbean" and "Beethoven's Fifth Symphony." They gave endless pleasure to their friends and family by highlighting each significant event of their lives with music and filling the air with happiness, joy, and hope. They were tagged as the "Adorable Music Couple" and no party was complete without them. However, their favorite song was, "Through the Fire and Flames" and they swore to abide by it whenever life might test them.

Unfortunately, that single fateful incident had set all of their promises and commitments aflame. Only a very delicate thread was holding them together now. To Darci, that fragile thread was the last remaining fragment of their love. Lennard had not actually bothered to ponder over it until now. He breathed deeply to keep himself focused on his goal and remain rooted in the present moment. He was aware that he had to embark on this journey himself and take full responsibility. He wanted to say so many things to his wife. He wanted to apologize for his indifference, and he wanted to give her a reason for his insensitivity over all these years, but he was fighting himself from within. The fight within was taking a toll on his body. A severe headache began to pound into his skull, and his vision turned blurry. He started to panic and shouted for help. The nurse was quick to arrive, and take him to his bed. He was fed, and medicines were administered, and before he could even be asked to rest for the evening, he had fallen into a deep sleep.

Raj finished his meal and asked Meera if she would like to spend some time alone. Meera's nurse helped her into her wheelchair, and soon the lovers were sitting hand in hand in their respective wheelchairs. The scenario was far from romantic or ideal, given how they were stiffly bandaged up, but they still had smiles on their faces. The comfort of holding each other's hands after such a grueling past seventy-two hours was priceless. They were so grateful to have each other after undergoing such a horrific turn of events. They discussed Darci and Peter and hoped and prayed for a happy turnaround for all of their tourist friends, as well as the driver. After those hopes and prayers, they were tucked into their respective beds.

Suddenly, there was a commotion in the middle of the night. A nurse crept into the ward and walked towards Lennard's bed. She touched him gently, to which he murmured, "Not now, Darci. Go to sleep."

She was taken aback and gulped and tried to speak, but something choked her. She patted his back again and bent towards his ear and said something, which made him jump up in his bed alarmed with a loud shriek.

Raj was quick to intervene, "What happened, Lennard?"

"Darci's vitals are dropping. We need Lennard to be there for the worst!" cried the nurse, unable to contain herself in such a tense situation.

Raj could feel a lump in his throat that refused to go down even after several gulps. Everyone had woken up after hearing the nurse, and for once Carl did not even curse. Everyone's faces were pale. Ira gasped aloud while Meera closed her moist eyes and Asha was quick to clasp her hands in prayer. Raj offered to go with Lennard to the ICU, but Lennard was ready to deny him in a gentle tone. Lennard was shaky at first, but then gathered his thoughts and then requested to be wheeled to the dreary room where his better half was laying motionless, surrounded by medical tubes and machinery.

Silence hung in the ward as he was leaving. Ira had her fingers crossed and could not resist shouting out, "Good luck!" to which Lennard was quick to request the nurse to pause the wheel of transport. He twisted himself around to make eye contact and whisper a quick thank you.

Sometimes when a man reaches a junction in life where he has nowhere to go, he tends to pause, reflect and absorb as many best wishes he can with the hope for the event to turn around. Hope is not just a noun that people use to address the many issues, but it is also an anticipation that man clings upon when the path seems dark with no place to go. Lennard was going through that phase in life. He was scared to tread that path, but he had no choice since he could not leave Darci alone. He took a deep breath before he was taken in, and upon seeing the doctor's expression he choked.

"Her vitals are sinking," uttered the on-call doctor with concern.

"What's your plan of action?" Lennard was quick to ask.

"We have paged the specialist and are waiting for his arrival. In the meantime could you please help by telling her some comforting words?"

Lennard began to sweat and the thought of being in the present and letting go of the past gave him a peculiar pain in his heart. He paused for a long time before nodding awkwardly. His unusual hesitance made the doctor a little confused. He left Lennard at her bedside and beckoned the nurse to follow suit.

"Hi, honey, how are you doing?" Lennard attempted weakly. Seeing no response, he sighed. Then he whispered those three words into her ear, and surprisingly, he saw a reaction. That made him jump up with mixed feelings. He could not believe it, so he tried it once more. The heart monitor began to beep louder and faster, and before he could even turn to call the nurse, the doctor came running in.

"What did you do?" asked the doctor anxiously

"Nothing, I just said a few words to her! What happened? Is she okay?" He wheeled himself out of the way to let the doctor examine Darci. The nurse was paged and they both began pushing some buttons on various machines while tilting the bed a little up to help her with breathing. "What is happening?" Lennard shouted while pulling his hair and rubbing his hands together. Anxiety spells can take a toll on the man, and if he does not channel it properly, stress tends to accumulate.

Lennard had usually been wise about knowing when to drain his excess pressure. He had found ways to do so with all these years of remaining in a tense and strained relationship with Darci over what she considered a "silly" argument. But the abortion had meant a lot to him and he just could not give in, not yet.

Then Lennard saw that Darci was twisting her shoulders and her eyelids were fluttering. The nurse was quick to remove the ventilator. Seeing that, Lennard brushed the nurse aside gently and came towards her bed, "Darci... Darci, how are you?"

Darci slowly opened her eyes. Her instant smile was captivating. The doctor and nurse were thrilled with this response from her and showered her with excited praise. Darci had always been a lover of life. She had no inhibitions and always found it comfortable to express herself. This captivated any onlooker and honestly made Lennard a little insecure. This time, however, he smiled back at her with moist eyes and kissed her hand gently. "It's good to have you back," he said with a deep tone.

"Oh! I had to come back, for you and for us," she whispered breathily. Her attitude was so refreshingly romantic that it caused tears to well up in the nurse's eyes.

"No one can take the spirit of this woman away. It was as if the drugs were confining her to a deep slumber and keeping her from living life on her own terms." The nurse whispered into the doctor's ear, to which he readily nodded.

Darci was making efforts to speak and that was making the machines beep faster since her vitals were getting jumpy. The doctor advised her to take it slow and she nodded, but after a minute she grew impatient again. "I hope that now we can have our 'happily ever after?'" Darci looked at Lennard expectantly.

Lennard looked at the floor, unable to create an eye contact. This made Darci grow uneasy. She repeated her question, this time a little louder than before. The machine's noises made the doctor and nurse anxious, and they began patting her shoulders and trying to calm her down. In an attempt to steady her heartbeat, the nurse butted in, "Oh yes, of course there will be a 'happily ever after.' Why wouldn't there be, Darci?" However, Mrs. Jensen wanted to hear reassurance from Lennard, who was still fighting the pain of letting go. He was in so much pain that he was practically deaf to the desperate pleas of his wife. Darci tried to touch his arm, but that stretch created chaos from the machines, and she let her arm fall limply back to her side. The nurse was surprised by Lennard's lack of reaction, despite how chaotic the room was, with machines beeping and hospital staff clamoring to attend to Darci.

Seeing the coldness coming from Lennard, Darci grew quiet and closed her eyes, though tears were trickling down her cheeks. The nurse beckoned to the doctor, as Darci's heart rate was sinking. The nurse smacked Lennard's thigh, gesturing to him to say something. She could not help but shout sarcastically, "Hey! Where are you? What are you dreaming about? Wake up!" as she waved her hands in front of his face.

Lennard had sweat running down his temples. He was trying hard to stay in the moment, but nobody else was aware of the internal struggle that he was fighting. Sometimes when a condition gets out of hand, even a stranger can show her affection by being aggressive without any remorse. The nurse was doing exactly that. She had no regrets about being outright rude to Lennard since even though they were used to facing death on a regular basis, the medical staff made sure they did not let any patient give into death so easily, at least not without a fight. The nurse was bent on doing whatever she could to help Lennard do his part in saving Darci.

Then the specialist arrived. He was very curious upon hearing that the patient was awake. He studied her vitals and scratched his beard, "With the kind of vitals she has been showing, I am very curious as to how she even regained consciousness," he whispered in the doctor's ear.

The nurse was quick to loudly inform him that the husband had whispered some magic words into her ear. She hoped that this would spur Lennard into repeating that act again. Lennard smiled at the nurse to let her know that he appreciated her gesture. That gave the nurse another chance to repeat herself while tapping his shoulder in a kind way. "What has gotten into you, sir? This is no time for daydreaming. Your wife was asking you a question. Couldn't you have just nodded, or said yes? Now you *need* to revive her. Make this doctor believe in miracles."

"I'm sorry, but I just cannot do it."

"What do you mean you *cannot*?" she put her hands on her hips with a perplexed expression. Even though Lennard's head was down, her constant gaze was burning Lennard's neck and he tried twisting his head back and forth to ease the burn.

Finally he uttered while giving a quick glance to her and then looking down at the floor again, "She wants me to forgive her for the past, and make a fresh start." He paused, and then after a deep breath continued, "But I cannot!" He looked up at the nurse to gain some sympathy, but she was just staring at Darci's vitals. The nurse shouted loudly to the doctor, who was studying Darci's file with the specialist on the other side of the room. They both walked briskly towards the bed. The doctor looked at the heart monitor and gasped while the specialist just twisted his lips into a silent sneer. Such circumstances were everyday occurrences for him. He had learned to embrace death and misfortune. Then he looked at the husband, who had grown panicked, seeing the staff circle around his wife. "What's going on? Is she okay?" Lennard became panicked.

The nurse avoided his eyes, refusing to reply.

The doctor focused on injecting something in her IV, in the hope of reviving her.

Finally, it was the specialist who spoke up. "I am afraid she only has a few minutes left. If you want to say something to her, now's the time."

Lennard's face was red, and he tried hard to tell something to Darci, but the right words were escaping him. He choked, perspiration flowing down his temples. He brushed his hands against his gown as if to gain control over himself. "Doc, can't you do anything about it? Please save my Darci!"

To which the nurse was quick to interject, "Then just forget and forgive the past, and say those words!" The doc and the specialist observed skeptically as Lennard picked up Darci's hand and kissed it gently.

"Darci, are you listening?" he asked in a gentle tone. "You can't leave me alone. Please don't go."

The nurse clucked disapprovingly, shook her head ruefully, and then looked towards the doctor with a defeated expression.

The machine started making loud noises as if bidding its farewell to the patient. Soon the machine that was pumping oxygen into her system stopped sucking and it lay still.

The nurse gave out a loud shriek. She had been in this profession for over a decade, but she had not yet been able to embrace death the way the specialist did. The doc signaled her to exit, to which she immediately obeyed, leaving the other three alone with the body.

Death is decided by the soul whose casing is the body. When a soul finds the body can no longer fulfill the purpose for which it developed the body, then it leaves the body and that is death. In Darci's case, she had tried to live her life in happiness, with the hope of reuniting with her lover one day. She had ached for a happily ever after with him since High School, but the incident in their mid-twenties took the joy out of their marriage thus, making this couple mature early in their lives. Her journey to Agra was a mutual decision by the couple, who both secretly longed to re-unite. Lennard had wanted to reconcile, but when it came to dissolving his past, he just could not bear the burden of letting go. Darci's soul had nothing else in store after that, so she had to let go of her body.

The specialist walked towards Lennard. "Mr. Jensen, we tried our best to revive her, but somehow she bruised internally and lost too much blood to come back. In fact, I was surprised that she even regained consciousness at all. And I was hoping for a miracle." With a gentle smile he continued, "Science and miracles usually don't go together, unfortunately." He sighed and patted Lennard's back, then walked out of the room. The doctor followed him.

Lennard remained staring at Darci, in awe and he could not move his eyes off her. In a few seconds, the tears started flowing. Tears usually flow when the heart becomes so full that it melts through the eyes. At such moments, the mind does not know what is going on and just goes out of the picture. There is a time of singularity with what is in front of one's eyes. Lennard was experiencing the above. He was gradually coming to terms of what lay in front of him, and after gently shaking Darci a few times to coax her to wake up, he gave up on it. He began crying loudly like a baby, his head resting upon her limp arm.

News spread quickly to the ward. All the patients pleaded to be wheeled into the ICU. At first the doctor objected to it, but then he realized that they all needed closure and healing as well. So he caved in and he gave the green light. Raj was the first one to enter, and he could not believe his eyes. Darci's body was cold and lifeless. He was used to seeing her jumping and laughing. The sight of her in her final state made him pinch himself so hard that his eyes grew moist, but he quickly wiped the tears away as his wheel chair was placed next to Lennard, whose head was still on Darci's arm. Raj placed his hand over Lennard's back and patted it gently. Lennard sat up and upon seeing Raj; he began to cry even louder. Sometimes, the sight of a compassionate face during a tragedy allows us to unload all of our grief in front of them.

Raj had become such a figure. He was a person that the tourists trusted and who they felt like they could turn to, confide in, and lean upon, both physically and metaphorically. For instance, here was Lennard, pouring out all of his sorrow to a person whom he had known for less than a week. Raj let him unload his grief while remembering the interactions he had had with Darci. He felt that she had left too soon. He had actually hoped that the Jensen's would reunite again, but even he could not override anybody's destiny. As he wiped his damp eyes, the others entered.

Asha motioned the nurse to stop at the entrance and she closed her eyes and started chanting. She had seen death before and her heart was still raw from her husband's demise. Prayers usually helped her stay strong.

Ira was holding hands with Meera as they entered. Seeing Darci's body, she immediately let go of Meera's hand and gasped loudly. She covered her mouth to avoid any noise, but her tears could not be controlled. Meera saw her, and got emotional too. She held onto Ira's wheelchair's armrest to steady herself. Seeing the peaceful look on Darci's face made her wonder if she was still playing games with them since she could never actually sit still. The incident when she rushed to skinny dip in the Taj Mahal waters came flashing back to her, and suddenly Ira's sobs turned into uncontrollable laughter, which garnered some odd looks from the others in the room, however, they were too engulfed by sorrow to question her.

When Carl's wheelchair was brought in, he took note of the intensity in the room and requested that his nurse parks him next to Asha's chair. Although he was an old man and many people in his life had died, Carl had always avoided attending funerals. He merely requested that his assistant send flowers and a card in his stead. So this time, seeing a dead body made him extraordinarily anxious. Witnessing Asha's closed eyes and crossed hands, he noticed that she was running her fingers over some beads. That made him curious, but upon seeing the calm expression on her face, he decided to save his questions for later. Instead, he gently touched her hand in a sign of support.

This trip had made Carl look within himself and put his ego aside. Lately, he had been curious about the changes that were occurring within himself, but upon finding peace through his new kind of thoughts and actions, he decided not to second guess himself. Carl found peace in following Asha's mannerisms and that was why his new self preferred to be around her.

The nurses left the grieving patients alone with Darci's body for a short while so that they could mourn their lost companion. Each traveler silently recounted their memories of joyful Darci, and many a tear was shed around the room. Those minutes seemed to pass by sooner than anybody expected, and soon the nurses returned to take them all back to their respective beds.

As soon as they reached their ward, the doctor came rushing in. He approached Raj and whispered something in his ear. Raj took a deep breath and closed his teary eyes. Meera caught his reaction and wheeled slowly towards him. Lennard also picked up on the stress in Raj's face and opened his mouth as if to inquire about it. Using only his eyes, Raj signaled to her that she should wheel herself towards his end of the room. Meera and Raj had been seeing each other for a few years, and she knew all of his moods and expressions to a tee. She immediately understood that it was something that Raj did not want Lennard to hear, so she obediently hurried to meet him.

Raj leaned in closely and whispered the words into Meera's ear.

Tears started trickling down her cheeks. Ira was watching with a keen eye and could not resist raising her eyebrows in concern and mouthing the words, "What's wrong?" to her friend Meera, whom she had gotten quite close to since the accident. Meera whispered something into Raj's ear and he nodded, so she beckoned Ira to come over. Ira hurried over, burning to know what was upsetting the two of them so much.

The sudden influx of people to one corner of the room caught Asha's attention. She looked up and even though her beads were still moving rapidly, her eyes were fixed intently on Raj's expressions.

Carl was equally interested and glanced at Asha. She shrugged back at him.

When Ira reached the couple, they quietly told her the news and she shrieked loudly. Asha could not contain herself any longer, and inquired loudly as to what all the commotion was about.

"Peter is awake! Peter is awake!" Ira announced loudly. Meera and Raj tried to shh her while looking towards Lennard compassionately.

It can be a very awkward situation when life and death meet at the same crossroads. Many people find it difficult to embrace one person's life when they are also saying their goodbyes to another. Everyone's eyes widened. Even Lennard was quick to look up and exclaim, "Oh!" His expression made it clear that he was thinking of Darci and hoping that some leftover magic might be sprinkled on her too, and then with a poof she could also join the club. Ira noticed his expression and decided to show some tact.

Ira requested that she be taken to Peter's room. Her urge was so honest and sincere that the nurse nodded with empathy and wheeled her into his room. "Only five minutes. Okay?" the nurse advised, as she parked Ira's wheelchair next to Peter's bed. Ira only half-nodded, completely distracted by the sight of a wide-eyed Peter, who was trying to answer some simple questions from the doctor to check up on his memory.

Upon seeing Ira, Peter turned towards her and smiled

"How are you?" she asked, brushing a few stray golden locks of her hair behind her ear.

Peter was taking his time to reply, so she jumped right into another question. She knew that the nurse would come back soon to take her back to her ward, so she wanted to make the most of this visit. She gently reached for his hands and placed them on her cheek, "You know I missed you so much, Peter. I never realized the impact of your absence until you actually became silent." Ira professed, tears streaking down her cheeks. Her confessions were loud and crisp, especially after having just encountered death in the next room. She knew now that she wanted to make use of her life to the utmost.

Peter nodded with teary eyes, as he stroked the soft skin of her cheek.

The doctor waited patiently, observing the couple and then glancing over into the next room where another couple had just separated. He sighed at the complexity and irony of life as he scribbled something on his notepad.

Their five minutes flew by, and the nurse returned promptly. She wheeled a teary Ira out, pacifying her by promising that she would be allowed to visit Peter again soon. Just as Ira was being wheeled out, Raj came in with the help of another nurse. He looked at Ira's expressions and winked at her. Ira did her best to smile back, despite her turbulent heart.

"Hey, Peter!" Raj announced loudly.

Peter was staring up at the ceiling fan with wide eyes and smiling. He tried to get up, but the doctor pressed down his shoulders, urging him to take it easy.

As Raj was wheeled towards Peter's bed, he winked at him with shining eyes. "You had us worried, man!" he said as he extended his hand to him. "Welcome back!"

At first, Peter stared at Raj's hand, then he extended his hand to engage in a handshake. He smiled and took a while to respond, but he was very expressive. That made the doctor happy and hopeful as he quietly added to his notes from the other side of the room.

Raj intervened, "Doc, how long before my bandages come off? I feel sorry for these poor nurses who are forced to chauffeur me everywhere." He smiled cheekily at his nurse, who smiled back.

"Soon, Raj," responded the doctor, with a gentle smile. "However, you need to rest enough for it to heal."

Raj nodded and requested the nurse to take him back to his bed.

Soon Asha, Carl, and Meera were wheeled in. They greeted Peter, expressed their happiness at his improved condition, and within minutes were transported to their respective beds. It had been a tiring day and they all needed their rest.

Once they all had left, the doctor announced that his visiting hours were over and it was time for him to rest. "Who were all those friendly people?" Peter stuttered, to the doctor while scratching his chin.

The doctor had been checking on his drip and was taken aback by his question. Wide-eyed, the doctor took a flashlight to examine Peter's eyes, and then paged the nurse while making some additional notes. After patting Peter's shoulder with a concerned expression, he gave the nurses some additional instructions and headed out for his next round of patients.

Lennard had returned to Darci's bedside. It was getting late, and a nurse named Shah came to wheel Lennard back to his bed, but he refused to leave Darci. He started to wail like a baby and the nurse was petrified. She immediately paged the doctor, who came in and tried reasoning with Lennard. Eventually, Lennard gave in and agreed to make arrangements for Darci's body. The doctor suggested that she be kept in cold storage so that Lennard could bury her in his hometown, and he gratefully agreed.

Shah overheard all of the details of their conversation, and thought to herself, *He was so hesitant to say, "Yes" to her "happily ever after." Now, I wonder what he will do with her tombstone in his town. It would have been better if he had just made amends with her when she was still alive. He is probably doomed to live a suffocated life!* Shah pitied him and hoped for a bright life.

Once all of their patients were in their respective beds, the doctor wiped his brow and seated himself in his clinic. Nurse Shah came in to get the necessary paperwork signed for Darci's body. Upon seeing the doctor in such a pensive mood, she inquired about it. Their remote hospital had never seen so many foreign patients, so for a moment she thought he was just tired or overwhelmed, but she was shocked to hear what the doctor had to say. She seated herself on a chair without taking his permission and started taking deep breaths. At that moment in time, her arthritis in her knee was not bothering her as much as the news. "So, we ought to find another specialist, now?" she remarked.

"Yes, I think so." The doctor opened his diary and started looking under "Mental Health."

"Can I go and take a look at him, Doctor Batra?" she asked.

"Sure, be my guest." He said while shrugging his shoulders as he sifted through the diary's pages.

Nurse Shah handed the signed papers to the morgue director, giving him permission to take Darci's body and preserve it until Lennard was ready to take it with him to Copenhagen. Then she gradually crept into Peter's room, where he was laying down, staring at the ceiling fan. As soon as he heard some footsteps, he tried to get up, while shouting a loud, "Hello!" He was desperate for company since his mind was empty, and he was getting bored.

"Well hello to you too," Nurse Shah said in a pleasant voice, trying to keep her composure as much as possible.

"Who are you?" asked the curious patient.

"I am a nurse here. You may address me as Nurse Shah." She said while standing near him, and checking his vitals.

"Nurse… Shah…" he repeated. "Okay! Nice to know one name. Where are all those other people?" he asked with a frown.

"Which people?" she inquired gently as she fidgeted with her pen.

"Those people… who came in wheelchairs." queried Peter

"Oh, those were your friends from the bus. They were all involved in the accident, and they came to meet and greet you when they heard that you had woken up."

"Bus? Which bus? Accident?" Peter was perplexed by the nurse's reply. Instead of answering, she changed the subject.

"What is your name?" she asked. The nurse swallowed a lump in her throat as she waited patiently. Peter scrutinized the fan as if the answers to her questions were hidden between its spinning blades.

"Peter!" he managed finally, raising his eyebrows and scratching his chest.

The nurse kept her vigil and nodded. Then she wrote down her observations. Just then, the pantry cart arrived with some food. Nurse Shah took a tray for Peter and helped him sit up.

The patient's eyes popped out seeing that food, and he ate with delight as the nurse watched him.

Occasionally, the nurse would quiz him about what he was eating, and he would pause from his chewing to answer. Nurse Shah was relieved that at least he still knew the correct names of the Indian dishes he was eating. Once the tray was put away, she helped him clean up, gave him his medicines and tucked him in. "You should rest now," she said with a smile of affirmation.

"Okay, Nurse Shah," Peter replied obediently.

The nurse stepped out of his room, took a deep breath and shook her head as she walked back towards the doc's office, "All is not lost. He has his old memories to accompany him. Besides, he is young and can make new memories. I am sure there is hope for him still. Thank heavens!"

Say Something

Doctor Batra made a few calls and got assurances that two specialists were going to visit him the next morning. He enjoyed a quiet meal before heading to the general ward where the other patients would be eager to know about Peter's condition, and would have to choose his words carefully in order to keep their recoveries going smoothly.

His patients were getting ready to be tucked in when the doctor arrived with a pensive yet steady smile. "Good evening to you all!" he tried to be as cheerful as possible. These people had faced both death and life in the span of a few hours, and the only way to greet them was with a smile.

"How is Peter?" asked Ira with an apparent sense of urgency.

After adjusting his collar and his coat, he smiled and pulled a chair into the middle of the ward so that he could address the group easily as a whole. "Well, I have something important to share about that." He took a deep breath. "Peter is fine. All of his vitals are working as expected. However, he is suffering from retrograde amnesia. What I mean by that is that he has lost his memory, most importantly his recent memories... including the memories he had created with all of you." The doctor paused and looked around the room, trying to gauge the reactions of the others before continuing. "But these are just memories, you see. He can always create new ones with all of you. What is most important is his physical health, and that is improving significantly with each day." He fervently wished that this negative turn of events wouldn't cause so much stress that it would set back the other patients' recoveries. He was of a strong belief that healing occurs only when there is peace within.

Surprisingly, none of the patients seemed to have anything to say. They were too bewildered by the unexpected news. The doctor looked at Ira, who seemed to be deep in thought. He wanted to go near her bed to comfort her, but he wasn't sure of the right words to say, so after giving a final look at Raj, he got up from his chair and started walking towards the exit.

"Just a minute, Doc!" piped up an unfamiliar voice. The doctor turned quickly towards it, and was surprised to find who had asked the question.

His eyes widened with curiosity and he answered, "Yes, Carl?"

"How can a man lose his present memory and keep his reminiscences intact? It's like me forgetting Barbara while choosing to keep Liz in my memories, and becoming, even more, bitter that she cheated on me."

"Yes, that would have been very unfortunate, Carl. But fortunately, Peter seems quite at peace with his past." the doctor took a deep breath and continued, "However, we will know more once the specialist examines him." He paused, waiting for any more questions, especially from Raj or Ira. But, to his surprise he found the guide in a pensive mood with his eyes transfixed on Meera.

Ira had decided to lie down, pulling her sheet over her head, a clear sign that she did not want to be disturbed. Shrugging, the doctor let himself out quietly.

The lights went out, and the shifts changed. Doctor Batra was reviewing paperwork in his office when he heard a loud voice come from the ICU ward. He was taken aback, and rushed towards the ICU, followed by the night shift practitioner. The door was half closed, and he could hear a man and a woman's voice arguing on the other side. He entered swiftly without knocking, and after taking a deep breath, placed a gentle hand on the woman's shoulder. She was standing with the help of her crutches, and she awkwardly spun around, giving him a guilty look.

Doctor Batra raised his hand as if he understood her feelings, and commented, "Arguing with him will not bring back his memories of you, Ira," he explained sympathetically.

"You don't understand, Doc! I was banking so much on this relationship. It was not just for my closure but also an opportunity to open another door for me! And now this!" she rolled her puffy eyes, taking a seat on the edge of Peter's bed. The doctor consoled her in a calm voice, as she cried and complained. Peter listened to their conversation quietly, wishing that he could remember this strange and furious girl who cried, then yelled, then cried some more. The doctor tried to guide her towards the door, but she resisted. That brought a frown to Batra's forehead. He attempted to make her understand the situation, but she was determined to handle it her own way. "Just give me a few more minutes, Doc," she pleaded. "I promise I will come out on my own. I need closure too just so you know," she said while wiping her tears off her cheeks. The Doc rubbed his hand over his face, and stroked his hair, trying to put himself in her shoes. Ira watched the odd motions of his big brown hands and hoped that he would come to see it her way.

Finally, he made a decision and his hands stopped moving. "Five minutes, and that's it," he announced in a commanding tone as he strode out of the room.

Ira nodded with assurance and turned towards Peter. She looked at him with compassion, tears streaming down her face, as she sat on the edge of the bed. "Say something, I am giving up on you. You know I could have followed you anywhere." she sung, recounting the words of one of her favorite romantic pop songs, which felt entirely appropriate given the situation. She tried to slide closer towards him.

Peter was drowning in her words and her weepy eyes but was still unaware of where it all was going. He pushed his sheet down towards his chest and tried to sit up. Ira continued, "I was learning to live as I started to fall in love with you." she admitted, looking deep into his eyes. After seeing the little reaction from him, she concluded, "I will stumble and fall if you don't accept me." She looked to Peter for a response, and his expression was kind but confused. He still had no idea who she was. She could not believe her life had changed so soon, and as she wiped her tears, she slowly got up, leaning heavily on the crutches. Her final words before leaving the room were, "I am sorry I could not get to you at that epic time and place when you needed me. I will regret that for all of my life as I continue to love you and say goodbye." Then she walked out of the room without giving him a second glance.

A New Day Has Come

The patients in the ward were up and about early in the morning. They were excited because most of their plasters were coming off for the examination and that meant being one stage closer to liberation. Next, all they had to undergo was physical therapy. They were happy to exchange a few laughs here and there as they ate and ingested their medicine. Although at the back of Raj and Ira's minds, there was a lot going on. As always, Raj tried his best to stay in the present and to keep the group recharged and motivated. Doctor B was excited to see this batch of patients continue on to the next level of treatment, especially after seeing a couple of their friends suffer, so he checked in extra early and finished visiting his other patients before he reached their ward so that he could spend uninterrupted time with this special group. "Good morning!" he shouted as he entered.

The curtains were still drawn since the patients were freshening up with the help of their respective nurses. Most of them chimed along with the doc's morning wishes while Ira pretended not to hear him. Ira's attendant walked out with a tray, and the doctor took a deep breath. He was not anticipating that Ira would be his first patient of the day. He walked towards her bed with a forced smile. "How are you doing this morning, Ira?"

"What is so special about *this* morning?" came her blunt response.

"You will gain freedom from these bandages. That's what so special." the doctor replied with high spirits as he started to examine her foot while the nurse came in with the tool kit to cut open her plaster.

Ira ignored his cheerful words, lying motionless on her bed. Her eyes were fixed on the ceiling fan, which was moving in a leisurely manner. Sad thoughts entered her mind, so she shut her eyes quickly to keep her tears locked inside. The nurse watched her and then stroked her shoulder while uttering kind words to her.

She nodded back with a silent "Amen." Bolstered by the nurse's affection, she began, "So, how does my foot look, Doc?"

"Last X-ray showed complete healing. However, I will be moving your foot back and forth. Please let me know if it hurts." he advised.

She nodded while taking a deep breath. He examined her and she complained of some stiffness. The doctor was satisfied since that was what he was expecting. He paged the therapist and discussed the issue with her while leaving for the next patient. The therapist introduced herself as Sunitha to Ira and exchanged a few words of wisdom with regards to her treatment. Ira complimented her jewelry and that initiated further friendly conversation. Sometimes a few words of flattery can break boundaries of any kind, leading to an unexpected friendship.

The doctor continued with his rounds, happy to open up bandages on Carl, Asha, Meera, and Lennard. Sunitha followed him around, making careful notes of what the patients' issues were and how to treat them. Finally, they reached Raj's bedside. Raj was still in fear of what might happen next for his friends. The fact that they had lost Darci, and now Peter as a friend, would not let him sleep at night, and it showed on his face. The doctor noticed his weary and anxious expression, and while examining Raj's ankle and knees, commented, "I wish life was practical. I would have loved my job every day."

Raj frowned and did not hesitate to counter argue, "Your career demands that you must be practical, but not mine. I am just supposed to bring happiness into people's lives, and depart from them after creating only fond memories. Why me?" he asked dejectedly.

Doctor Batra paused in action, giving a tender and knowing smile to Raj.

Raj was an emotionally intelligent being, and he immediately understood the meaning of the doctor's grin. He raised his hands and stroked his head gently, "Yeah! I know where you will be going with this, Doc. But I did not want this for my tourists!"

"Sure, I understand. But you aren't the one who decides their fate," said the doctor, resuming his work.

"I could have been more careful, though. That accident could have been avoided."

"Accidents are termed as unexpected. Nobody wants to be hurt."

A therapist, who popped in and began asking Raj about his pain and discomfort, interrupted their conversation. Then the doctor got a page, and he excused himself from the ward. Sunitha gave a brief schedule to all her patients and then exited with the nurse. Silence filled the room afterwards, but Raj was not afraid to break it.

"So, aren't we glad to have come to the last phase of our recovery, huh?" he began, trying to put some optimism in the air.

Carl was quick to respond in a jubilant tone, which was followed by Asha's agitated cry for Kamala. By this time, all in the room knew about each other and the names that impact each other's lives, thus Meera could not help but chuckle at Asha's lament.

The cheerful giggling was interrupted by a flat and cold voice. "When can I go home with Darci?" asked Lennard. A chilling silence entered the room.

Raj was quick to chip in, "It depends on the opinion of the physical therapist, Lennard. How soon can you move around without pain?"

"You mean physical pain? Because the mental pain refuses to leave," said Lennard sarcastically.

Meera was quick to interject in a gentle, but blunt voice, "As long as you have memories of Darci, the mental pain will always be there, Lennard."

Carl was in another world and did not care about the strained atmosphere, "I was wondering if I could Skype with Barbara and show her my latest self." That was more of a suggestion than a question, so Raj had to comply with it. He nodded and beckoned the nurse to arrange an Internet session. In what felt like no time, Carl was joined with Barbara via a computer screen.

The road to recovery was moving faster than expected. The patients were first seen limping around the ward and around their beds, but gradually they were enjoying the outdoors with a cane, which lightened their moods and brought smiles to their faces. On many occasions, Ira would be seen wearing a broad beam, although she kept trying to peek into the ICU with the hope to catch a glimpse of her past. Asha started on the road to walking with limps and the regular chanting of Kamala's name, but gradually as hours went by, she seemed to become more and more confident. Carl's shoulder and toe were doing much better, and he would occasionally refrain from his daily doses of painkillers, which was a surprise for the docs who complimented him on that decision.

Lennard would be seen sitting outside near the fountain, enjoying the occasional cool spray falling on him, and reminiscing about Darci, who could not stand the heat and loved such fine mists on her skin. His body ached as his heart cried over her loss, but he had to continue with his life. He had no choice!

Raj would take turns to stroll around with his tourists, who had become more like family for him. Family meant a lot to him. Unfortunately, he did not have one of his own, and the fact that these individuals who surrounded him had high regards for him despite what had happened, made him feel even closer to them. He wanted only the best for each one of them. Meeting with Asha and Carl was always quick. They were eager and restless to get home. Carl wanted to reunite with Barbara and bring their family back under one roof, while Asha wanted to get back to being pampered and nursed by her live-in maid. She was also keen to jot down her experiences so far during this trip. With age, her memory can sometimes slow down, and that fear was making her anxious. She had promised to deliver on time, handing over a bunch of information that would become top-notch news. Such news could either bring down an empire or throw some limelight on an issue that needed extra attention. Raj was curious and wanted to know more about this information, but she preferred to remain secretive about her notes, always changing the topic. Raj got the hint, and let that issue go.

When Raj met with Ira, there was silence at first, and then they both wept since they had lost somebody dear to their hearts. Peter had no recollection of either of them, thereby making Ira and Raj the same as any other unknown face that he might encounter on the street one day. Both of these individuals had fond memories of him. About two years ago, to Raj, he was an ex-neighbor that turned into a dear friend who would always be at his beck and calls while Ira had desperately wanted to make something special out of their relationship. But now everything had been erased except their memories. They both felt each other's pain, and they spent some time reminiscing about Peter sharing soft cries and chuckles. "I am sorry you had climbed the ladder of a different relationship with Peter. I wish I could have seen the future so I could have warned you to be more careful." Raj said, patting Ira's shoulder gently.

Ira wiped her tears and swayed her head from left to right. This swaying of one's head was something she had learned from the locals. They would bend, swing, nod their heads frequently, and she used to like how expressive they were even in their body language, and she had quickly grown fond of it, just like how she had grown fond of Peter. "I wish I knew it too, Raj. I was so oblivious to my real feelings for him that I did not realize how I really felt until he was not around." She inhaled deeply, and continued, "Maybe, I still wanted to hang on to my past... so I could not carve out a road map with the new Peter. Instead, I just used him until he dropped me like a hot brick." They both chuckled over the hot brick, and Raj could not resist commenting.

"You know, hot potatoes are yummier than hot bricks!"

That made Ira burst into laughter as she nodded her head in agreement.

Before leaving her company, Raj told Ira that their acquaintance with Peter would now be treasured even more, since he did not give a damn about them.

"I am sure you mean the Tinker Damn?" corrected Ira, in joking play on words. They both chuckled lightheartedly, and Raj was glad that Ira could smile again and be happy.

Raj finally got a chance to meet up with Meera after his next physical therapy session. The first thing he did was hug her tightly, and they stayed in that position for a long time. So long, in fact, that the nurses began staring at them, and Meera had to push him away since she was getting embarrassed. Raj did not feel the need to apologize. He looked at her tenderly and inquired about her healing process. Although, he was getting updates from the therapist, it seemed better to hear it from Meera's mouth. As she was demonstrating her movements, Raj could not resist getting close to her, and embracing her again. Meera initially held him, but as the seconds kept ticking, she felt the desperate need in his embrace and pushed him away gently, asking, "Are you okay, Raj?" She wore a concerned expression on her face.

"You know that you are a beautiful soul," he paused and continued, "Both inside and out. You are in fact, the complete package."

"Where are you going with this, huh?" Meera inquired with a grin.

Raj continued while holding one of her hands, "You know we have been in a relationship for over two years now."

"Umm two years and three months, to be precise, Raj." Meera said sternly but with a sly smile.

"Oh, my mistake! See, I always told you that you were good at math!" he joked while scratching his stubble and looking into her eyes, "But, you know I have even always loved your imperfections. Your—"

"Excuse me?"

"Let me continue, Meera. I mean your perfect imperfections. I love every single bit of you, your curves and edges and all that is yours. You have been my pillar of support throughout everything, and you are my end and my beginning." He swallowed a lump in his throat. "I love you! Marry me, Ms. Bhaskar!

Meera's eyes began to tear up, but she wanted those tears to stay put since they were in public, so she raised her eyebrows to avoid them from running down her cheeks. She was shocked by his request; since at the beginning of their relationship, he had made it very clear that he was not looking for marriage. He hadn't even given Meera any choice about it. At first, it had been tough for her to absorb the arrangement, but with time she had developed a peculiar kind of closeness with her beau that made her rely on him at any hour of the day. That sense of trust and assurance had given her the conviction that he would be hers until she breathed her last breath, even if she never had a piece of paper to prove it.

"Ummm… I don't know what has got into you, Mr. Malhotra," she began playfully, although her voice was choked with tears of joy. "Are you still taking those narcotics to subside your pain?"

"Nah! You know I left them long ago, ever since I started limping around the corridors of this hospital. I admit that when we met, I was not the kind of guy who wanted commitment. I still remember what I told you on our first night together, a couple years ago."

"Two years and three months ago!" Meera was quick to chip in.

"Aha! Yes, to be that precise!" he said while rolling his eyes.

"So, what made you change your mind, Raj?" asked Meera meekly, while placing her head on his chest as he embraced her from the side.

"This recent chain of events has made me feel like I need to let go of my fears. I have always had a fear of committing to a relationship because I want to avoid the sorrows that occur when life doesn't live up to your expectations." He paused, and put his head near Meera as a support and continued, "But if I don't let go of this fear, I will regret it when I am on my deathbed. And if I have that anguish and bitterness when I have only a few breaths left in this body, I will not be able to rest in peace. Thus, I have to do this for myself. I must take my destiny on a test drive, even though I know I told you that I didn't want to step into that zone, ever!"

Fear is one word that can be sensed from miles away. Unfortunately, Lennard was only a few feet away from this lovey-dovey couple. These days he admired peace, and wanted seclusion even more so he could calm his rattling nerves. When he heard the word "fear" he could not resist getting up, and walking towards them. He barged in with a sneer, "What are you fearful about Raj? Had I known you were so 'fearful' I would have thought twice about coming here in the first place? And the best part about that would be that Darci would still be alive and we could be in a similar pose like how you two lovebirds are!"

Hearing his harsh words, Raj and Meera disengaged from their cuddle, sitting up straight and keeping their hands to themselves. Raj was still digesting Lennard's words, but Meera was quick to respond in a raised voice, "You don't know anything about Raj and what he has been through! You have no right to judge him, or his fears!" Sometimes standing upright and talking in a loud voice can help intimidate another person, and that was Meera's motto. Lennard shirked back a few inches with a frown, still looking at Raj, who seemed to be deciding whether to confront him or let it go. Meera could read Raj's mind, and she answered him aloud, saying, "Raj, don't even think of letting it go this time. You ought to tell him your history, so he can learn from it and carry on with his life."

Lennard scratched his head in bewilderment, and could not resist parking himself on the bench opposite Raj.

Raj looked up with a frown while placing a hand on Meera's arm to calm her down. Then he faced Lennard. He looked at him expressionlessly, and continued, "Look, Lennard, I don't mean to be harsh to you, nor am I trying to teach you anything, especially after what you have been through. Your plate is already full, but since you have asked me about my fears and my past, I don't mind sharing it with you." He took a deep breath and brushed his hand over his face to prepare himself to safely dig deep within himself.

Meera scooted closer to him, gently placing her hand on his thigh for assurance.

Raj began, "The word 'family' does not sit well with me."

Lennard was confused and his eyebrows rose in surprise.

Raj grinned widely to hide his pain and elaborated, "As a kid, I lost my parents in an accident and was left an orphan. I grew up in an orphanage where I did my schooling, and once I got a job, I left that institution and settled on my own." He paused long hard as if trying to swallow the pain that came along with this mental rewind while placing his fingers over his eyes to keep them from swelling with tears.

Meera patted his leg gently, and he nodded to assure her that he was fine.

"I am sorry to hear about your loss, Raj. You went through quite an ordeal," Lennard offered apologetically.

"Thank you, but I wish that was the end of it, Lennard," said Raj promptly. "However, there is more. I was a happily married man with a corporate job, and I enjoyed all of the necessary comforts of life. Just then, fate got another chance to ridicule me. I lost it all. And when I say *all*, I mean that was left on the streets again with nothing."

Lennard's intense expression showed that he wanted to know the details of how it happened, but Meera was quick to intercept. "It does not matter how it happened, Lennard. The fact that it happened, and he could still stand up, walk like a man, and look eye to eye with all of us, tells a lot about him. Doesn't it?"

Lennard remained quiet, looking at Raj.

Hearing no response, Meera got irritated, and repeated, "*Doesn't* it, Lennard?"

"Oh! Yes. Yes, absolutely," he murmured obediently, still fixated on Raj, whose eyes were fixated on the ground. Sometimes, focusing on something can be therapeutic since it shuts down the physical self and helps an individual look inside and stabilize their thoughts. Raj was attempting to do just that. He mumbled something softly to himself, and Lennard had to concentrate to hear his words.

"Her name was Sheela, and we were married for one good year. We were thinking of starting a family when she was diagnosed with lung cancer, stage four." Tears were rolling down his cheeks while his eyes stayed focused on the floor. He continued, "I spent every dime I had on her treatment, but fate had something else in store for me." He was interrupted by another pat on his leg from Meera. He blinked, and looked up as if nothing had happened. Wiping away, his tears, and taking a deep breath, he smiled, with his hands raised towards the sky, "Destiny huh? No one can change it, so you just have to face it. However, the fear that was instilled in me from all those tragedies was something to be reckoned with, that's for sure! But no more! I'm finally moving forward."

Lennard nodded, then got up and walked towards Raj, silently embracing him in a warm hug. Raj was quick to reciprocate. As they hugged, Meera wiped her tears and clasped her hands together in gratitude.

"You have to keep rowing your boat, Lennard," advised Raj.

"Oh! Sure. But first I gotta find those oars, Raj."

Raj patted his back confidently, "You will. Be on the lookout, and you will."

Lennard headed back to his bed, leaving the two lovebirds alone again.

Once they were alone, Meera was quick to ask, "Are you okay?"

"I think so. My heart is still racing, but I'll be fine." He pressed his temples to ease his nerves. "I hope Lennard keeps my tale in his memory and brings it up whenever he is feeling down, to help him trudge along."

Meera nodded while hugging him tight. "You are a warrior, and that is the reason I love you."

"Yeah, about that..." Raj kissed her hands, and knelt down, "Are you going to marry me or not?"

"Are you really sure you are ready to do it?" inquired an ecstatic yet cautious Meera.

"Yes, I mean it. These past few weeks have given me an entirely new perspective on life. I realize that there is no greater gamble than living it all over again, even though I have lost it all twice. Call me crazy, but I am ready to roll the dice again!"

Meera got up and hugged him tightly. "And there is a magnificent chance that you will not lose this time! I have a good feeling that someday I will be reminiscing about this moment with our grandchildren!" Tears streamed down her cheeks.

They were locked in a teary embrace for quite some time, until Raj interrupted, "Err Meera, you still did not respond to my proposal."

Meera gave him a sidelong look, and kissed him on his cheek. That was followed by another long smooch. It was a passionate one and they were able to unload their mental stress and the constrictions that narrowed their perspective on life. So much had happened around them in the past few weeks. "You've got your answer now." Meera disentangled herself from him and then winked at Raj as she limped off down the corridor towards her bed.

The aching sadness he felt over losing Darci and Peter filled Raj with the urge to chase after her and hold onto her, never letting her go. But Raj knew there would be lots of time for that in the future. So he let her go with a sigh.

Forever Until Tomorrow

After a couple more days of rehabilitation, the patients were signing release papers. Raj took responsibility for the treatment expenses of all of his tourists and assured the staff that he would pay them in installments.

Lennard was happy to be leaving with Darci. Meera's colleague had helped with organizing and collecting the tourists' luggage while they were recovering in the hospital. He had also taken care of their bookings to go home. A courtesy bus from the hotel arrived at the hospital to pick up the group. Prior to boarding the bus, Ira and Raj made a quick visit to Peter's room, where they found him with his fingers interlocked with an unfamiliar but beautiful face. The two were deep in a charming conversation, whispering sweet nothings into each other's ears. Upon seeing the two unknown faces enter the room, the patient turned with an expression of surprise, while the young woman gave out a pleasant smile towards Raj. Peter did not hesitate to ask, "Do I know you?"

Ira just stood there staring at the cute lady, while waving goodbye to Peter with teary eyes.

Raj put his hand on Ira's shoulder, and whispered, "Let it go!"

Ira nodded and looked up at the ceiling to keep her tears from falling on her cheeks.

Raj echoed a soft goodbye while waving at Peter, and gave a teary wink at the damsel while whispering, 'Take care of him!' and then he dragged Ira along with him down the hallway.

That action left Peter puzzled, "Crazy people, huh? I wonder if they escaped from the mental health wing?" The beautiful lassie had wet eyes, and was shocked to see how memory loss can be so accurate while thanked it at the same time for it to be able to re-unite with her college sweetheart. She laughed and nodded in agreement, and they went back to their smooching and whispering.

Lennard was eager to get home and prepare for Darci's funeral. He had made the proper arrangements to take the coffin along. Everyone was there to see him off except Peter, and Ira was present physically but in a muted form. All of the travelers exchanged their goodbyes and their best wishes and promised to stay in touch via all sorts of technology. Raj double-checked that all of his information was saved in Lennard's contacts, just so that he could be of constant inspiration and keep him from getting discouraged along the rocky path of life. He was happy that he had opened his past to him, since it not only gave Lennard a way to introspect on his goals in life but also to help Lennard realize that a man is the strongest when he is at rock bottom. He can rise high if he chooses to! Raj smiled as they all waved at Lennard's departing plane.

Carl was also keen to jump on the flight back home, but for different reasons. Raj and Carl hugged each other at the departure lounge. "I hope to see you again, with Barbara," said Raj.

"Yes, definitely. We both must come visit next time, and I still have to finish this tour!" said a jovial Carl. Raj nodded and smiled, and then he turned around to leave. As he was walking away, he heard a voice from behind him. "You're a good man, Raj!" Raj turned around to see Carl waving at him again. The happy tour guide waved back.

Asha was next to leave, calling a cab to take her back to Delhi. She was all packed up and waiting for Raj and Meera in the lobby while scribbling frantically in a notepad. The couple noticed her frenzied actions from a distance and frowned. Meera approached Asha and gently stroked her shoulder. Asha looked up in shock and hurriedly threw her notepad into her purse with an awkward laugh. She had been so involved in her writing that she hadn't even noticed their approach. Meera was left confused and Raj didn't want to bother with any more questions, so he wished her luck and helped load Asha and her baggage into the cab.

"You will be hearing from me shortly, Raj," Asha assured him as she rolled down the window of her cab.

"That would be great. We should undoubtedly stay in touch!" replied Raj earnestly.

"Oh yes, we most certainly will!" exclaimed Asha with an odd smirk that gave Raj the shivers. After a few minutes, Raj shook that strange feeling away by embracing Meera as they walked towards the lounge of the hotel.

"Ira wants to stay for a few days," remarked Meera, "Having her stay in the hotel would be expensive, especially since this trip has already put a hole in your pocket. What should we do?"

"Can she stay with you?" asked Raj.

Meera paused and looked at him with a broad smile, "That is a brilliant idea. Let me ask her!" she dashed towards her room, leaving Raj in the lobby, where he sat down with a pile of papers in his hand.

After an hour or so, Ira and Meera came striding towards Raj. He was still working in a corner of the lobby with his hands on his forehead, trying to sort out his dues and balances. Their chirpy voices caught his attention, and he could not resist a smile upon hearing that Ira would be staying with Meera. Within minutes, Ira's bag was being loaded and she was being transported to a new address that would be much more comfortable than the hotel room.

Meera welcomed Ira to her abode. It would be Ira's home for the next few days. Ira looked around that cozy apartment and cooed in delight while Meera gave her details about her apartment. Meera showed her where to put her things. "Relax, take a shower, and I will be home in a few hours for dinner," Meera instructed, as Ira lay on the futon bed that was arranged for her.

"Sure thing. No worries!" smiled Ira.

Meera returned to work to find Raj eagerly waiting for her. "How about we get married next week?" he asked earnestly, and then continued with a smirk, "I have just enough funds left to take care of a simple wedding, and our honeymoon will consist of a luxurious week of being waited on hand and foot at my apartment by yours truly, of course."

Meera laughed out loud, and then covered her mouth out of modesty. After realizing what she just did, she could not resist in hugging her boyfriend, "Wow! Let's do it! I have microscopic time to shop for my wedding dress!" she blushed and called her mom to deliver the happy news, but she frowned at the response on the other side of the line, hanging up on a sour note. Raj's stomach sunk after seeing her expression and he hugged her to show his support. He promised her that he would discuss it with her later after work, and then he left to run some errands.

The news of Meera and Raj's betrothal spread quickly among the hotel staff. Well-wishers accosted Meera at every turn to congratulate her. She was enjoying the moment, and since she never dreamed that this day would come, she was filled with additional gratitude. The day went by quickly. Married women began giving her tips on where to purchase her trousseau, and she took earnest notes. She had plans to go right after her shift ended. In the midst of that happy commotion, her cell phone rang. It was Ira! With all this excitement, she had momentarily forgotten that she had a temporary roommate. She hung up, promising that she would be home in a few minutes. She told Ira to be ready to go out when she returned since they had important business to take care of together. Ira was confused, but Meera hung up without giving any further explanation. She wanted to tell her friend the good news in person.

After winding up her day at work, she drove home in a frenzy while cursing everyone who came in her way and did not spare her horn or accelerator. She couldn't wait to tell Ira the news. Finally she reached her apartment, and burst through the door, panting. Ira shrieked at her swift entry. Meera laughed and took a deep breath, apologized, poured herself some water, and plunked down on the couch next to Ira with a glass in her hand. She embraced her stunned friend in a warm hug, shouting, "Wooo!" in delight.

Ira pulled away and gawked at her with eyes wide open. *Meera indeed had gone mad!*

"Ira, would you like to be my bridesmaid?"

"Ahhh! Say what?" Ira could not believe what she was hearing, "You are getting married?"

"Raj proposed to me at the hospital. We will be getting married next week!"

"Wow! I am so excited to see a Hindu marriage!" squealed Ira in delight. "Yes! Yes! Yes!" That left Meera puzzled. Now it was her turn to be confused, as she watched Ira jumping around wildly in excitement while shouting affirmations. Then Ira paused, put her hair behind her ears, and responded maturely while taking in deep breaths, "Sure I would love to be a part of this special day of yours. Tell me, how can I help you?" Just then the phone rang, interrupting them. Meera raised her finger to silence her hyper friend and answered the call, her heart still beating loudly with excitement.

"Hi Raj," she said lovingly. Before she could continue, Ira snatched the phone away from Meera and congratulated the guide, then after exchanging a few chuckles, she gave it back to its rightful owner. "Sure, let's meet at the market in an hour's time. I have a few shops to window shop at first, so that should give us enough time to do so." Meera hung up and then the duo dashed outside. They hopped on Meera's motorcycle and were on their way.

Ira liked sitting on the two-wheeler as it dashed through the busy street, although she was extra cautious to keep her hands to herself, especially when they passed a cow or a dog that shared the road with the throngs of people. Once they reached their destination, they strolled around the various shops. Each store was filled from floor to ceiling with the vibrant colors of Indian attire. As Ira admired them, Meera focused on the price tags, often shaking her head in dismay. She was getting anxious since nothing even came close to fitting into her budget.

The thought of borrowing her mom's dress for her wedding entered her mind many times. Her mother had offered it to her a long time ago, but Meera did not have the guts to ask her about it. Her family had not taken well to Raj due to his aversion to commitment and the fact that he had already been married once before. It saddened her that her mother disapproved of the engagement, but she was not going to let that keep her from marrying the man she loved.

Time flew by fast as the girls shopped, and they soon reached the restaurant where Raj was supposed to meet them. Thinking again of her mother, Meera did not realize that her eyes were watering until Raj arrived and wiped her budding tears away. He hugged her gently, offering, "Let's go tomorrow to meet with your mom."

"I don't think she will ever understand, Raj. What's the point?" she mumbled into her damp wad of tissue. Ira sat next to her, putting her arm around her comfortingly.

"We can't fix anything if we don't try, Meera," said Raj. "Let's, at least, give it a shot." She nodded in agreement and called her mother, setting up a time to meet the next day. Then the three companions ordered dinner, enjoying a hearty and lavish meal to celebrate Raj and Meera's forthcoming union.

Night Changes

The trio stayed up late that night talking and planning for the wedding. Eventually, Ira could no longer keep her eyes open and Meera pushed Raj out of her home with the promise to see him next day. Even though it was late and Raj was tired too, he decided to take a detour on his way home. Soon he found himself knocking on his friend's door.

"Who's there?" came a curious voice that was mixed with fear and anger.

"Hi Lalit, this is Raj here!"

"Raj!" He opened the door and continued with an inquisitive tone, "What brings you here?" while moving aside for his friend to step in.

"I have come to make that paperwork official," Raj replied in a confident tone.

"Hmm… making the paperwork official, huh?" Lalit asked sleepily while scratching his back. He continued, "Raj, you actually love her, don't you?"

"Yes, I do." replied Raj with a smile, "Now, let's do it already."

"Okay, if you insist." Lalit sat down to type up a document that the two friends had discussed a long time prior. Within thirty minutes, he was finished. He printed the paper, stamped it, signed it, and handed the envelope to Raj. It was official! Raj hugged Lalit tightly prior to leaving.

"Good luck, my friend." Lalit shouted as he walked away, and Raj waved back with gratitude.

The next day, Raj arrived early at his fiancé's doorstep. Meera had gone home early from work in hopes of calling her mother to ease the tension, but it didn't seem to have helped at all. She was dreading her visit and had locked herself in the bathroom, taking deep breaths and preparing for what might happen once Raj arrived. "Meera! Raj is here!" Ira called, knocking softly on the bathroom door. "Are you okay?" Sensing the stress from the couple, Ira had opted to stay at home and let the couple have quality time with Meera's mom without her.

"Don't worry girl, I'm all right!" Meera pulled herself together, reapplying her lipstick and heading out to meet her betrothed. Ira gave her a hug and wished her luck before plopping down on the couch with some naan and chutney to catch some of her new favorite programs. She had come to enjoy subtitled Indian dramas and game shows and figured that would be a good way to pass the time until Meera returned.

The happy yet anxious couple reached Meera's mother's front door and took deep breaths to prepare themselves. The door displayed a brass tablet with an engraving that read "Mr. & Mrs. Bhaskar." Meera got emotional seeing the shiny plaque, envisioning her mom cleaning it religiously, despite her father's passing, years prior. Meera gathered her courage and knocked. There was no response. Immediately, Meera's heart skipped a beat. She had stopped visiting her mother ever since she had gotten serious with Raj. Each of her visits had resulted in an argument about Raj and his past, and eventually Meera just could not take it anymore. So she resorted to merely calling her mother from time to time. Meera began to grow teary, thinking about how much she loved her mom and wishing that somehow this issue could be resolved. She took a deep breath and called her mother, but got no response.

Sighing, she walked over to her neighbor's house to inquire. Upon finding out that her mother had been seen leaving to go to the temple, she breathed a sigh of relief. The couple settled in on the front steps to await Mrs. Bhaskar's return. While waiting, Meera noticed that Raj was holding an envelope. When she asked him what was in it, he replied, "You'll see."

After about an hour, a rickshaw came to an abrupt halt on the street in front of them, and an old lady with short grey hair exited the rickshaw in a feeble fashion. She haggled loudly about the fare with the driver, and then carefully began to walk in their direction, balancing a large plate with both her hands. Meera's eyes brimmed up with tears as she watched her mother struggle. Getting up, she cautiously hurried down the path to meet her elderly mother. She reached out, offering to help her mother carry the tray the rest of the way. At first, her mother adjusted her glasses to confirm what she was actually seeing, and then she squeaked in delight while extending her arms to embrace her daughter. Meera took the paten from her mother's hands, and then hugged her. They embraced for a few long minutes while tears gushed down both of their cheeks. Suddenly, the older woman noticed Raj in the distance, sitting on her front steps. She immediately let go of Meera. "What is he doing here?" she asked with a horrified expression.

"We have come to try to get your blessing, Mom."

Meera's mother waved her hands in the air as she brushed past her daughter, hurriedly limping the rest of the way to her front door. As she undid the top lock, she muttered, "I have no blessings for a man who is a walking curse for his friends and family!"

Raj and Meera exchanged worried looks on the doorstep as her mother made her way inside. Meera's eyes grew teary again, and she gripped the railing on the steps to steady herself. Raj placed his hand on her shoulder to help calm her down. His expression was calm and neutral, and Meera wondered how he could manage such a feat.

Bolstered by Raj's support, Meera followed her mother into the kitchen. "Mom, why do you say that?" she asked in a mellow voice. "Ever since Raj has been in my life, I have achieved nothing but success!"

Her mother turned back with a frown, giving her daughter a look that said, *You should know better!*

122

Meera continued with her explanation, "I started off as just an intern at the Taj, and now I have secured a hospitality position with a good enough salary to afford all of the modern conveniences that I might desire. Raj has supported me completely along the way, and without his love, I might have given up."

"Yeah, I have noticed that you had stopped asking me for money. That's good. I'm glad that you have achieved such success. But you are not the problem." Meera's mother declared as she put a pot on the stove, "My dear, you know about his past. So why are you bent upon shortening your life?" She began chanting, "Ram, Ram, Ram," while pouring milk and adding tea leaves to the boiling pot on the stove.

Meera disapproved of her mother's superstitions and scoffed though her eyes were yet again growing damp. "I am surprised that my mom, who was once a high school teacher, is now talking about all this superstitious rubbish." She crossed her arms and arched her eyebrows.

Her mother ignored her playful insult and continued in a raised voice, "Once you become a mother, you will understand what I am talking about."

Raj, who was still waiting outside on the doorstep, realized that the meeting was not going anywhere. So he entered and handed the envelope to Meera's mother. She gave him a dirty look, but when he beckoned for her to open it, she sat down on a kitchen chair, opening the seal.

When she saw the papers that were inside the envelope, she was puzzled, and expressed her bewilderment, "Adoption papers? What the heck is this?" she asked in a baffled and irritated tone. "Why would I adopt you? What would I get from this?"

Meera also gave a confused look to Raj.

Raj, on the other hand, was feeling very confident. He knew that this reaction would arise so he sat down next to Meera's mother to explain himself. "Mrs. Bhaskar, I am aware of my past, and, unfortunately, I cannot change it." Exhaling deeply, he continued, "My future lies with Meera, but because of my ugly past you have understandable concerns about how our future might turn out. So, after a lot of thought, I have decided to adopt your values, ideas and perception towards life with the hope that it will help change my future, which I believe could be my own 'happily ever after.'"

Tears began rolling down Meera's mother's face. She started justifying herself, "I didn't mean to be so harsh on you, but I hope you can understand where I am coming from." Meera's mother wiped her tears with the handkerchief that she always kept in her blouse sleeve.

Raj was prepared to give everything he had just to get blessings from Meera's mother, and that seemed to be just what was needed to prove his love for her. Meera hugged him tightly, and even her mother could not resist joining in. She hugged both of them, then showered them with the blessings they had craved. Within minutes, they were sharing jokes and laughter over tea.

When Meera's mother inquired about the wedding preparations, Meera was quick to ask, "Mom, I would be honored to wear your wedding dress for my special day... that is if your offer still stands." Meera smiled hopefully, but her heart was thumping with anxiety. *Please say yes, please,* she hoped, crossing her fingers beneath the table. Meera's mother could not help but blush. Then she stood up to retrieve the dress from her closet, which she always kept close at hand. Placing it in Meera's lap, she leaned down and kissed her daughter's forehead. The grateful twinkle in Meera's eyes made Raj beam. He was so glad that everything had gone according to his plan. Family was so much more important than money, and he just wanted to make sure that their wedding was as wonderful as possible for his beloved.

After finishing their tea, Meera and Raj prepared to leave. As they headed out the door, Meera's mother gave the envelope back to Raj. "I don't need this, but I actually appreciate the gesture. I am proud of you, and I wish you both well, always." Raj could not resist but hug her. For a minute, Meera's mother was frozen with shock, but she eventually cracked, breaking a smile and returning his embrace. Witnessing that touching moment, Meera's eyes grew moist again, but this time out of happiness.

No More Second Chances

Carl had texted Barbara prior to boarding his flight, and he simply could not wait for his plane to land at Frankfurt. During the trip, he kept reminding himself to be patient and understanding of those around him. He made his best efforts not to react negatively to minor mistakes made by the stewardesses and any annoying habits of the passengers around him. A baby was crying loudly in the coach cabin, and it was giving him a headache. The old Carl would have gotten up, stormed through the curtain separating first class from coach, and would have loudly berated the parent. This time, he simply opened a magazine and plugged in his headphones, putting some calming Jazz music on until the newborn stopped crying. As a result of his efforts to be "new and improved," his behavior on his flight home was commendable. He became acquainted with many of the travelers seated around him, due to his friendly behavior, and even the stewardesses occasionally stopped by his seat to chat with him.

Carl could see what a difference being friendly made in the way that others treated him. He was actually receiving better service from the stewardesses as a friendly passenger than he ever did when he was cold and rude! And when he was nice to others, they were so friendly in return. It felt good to be smiled at instead of glared at. In fact, it was so much more pleasant that he decided that the gains were definitely worth the extra effort. He chuckled quietly to himself upon realizing his folly. Had he known the benefits of making an effort to be friendly, he would have embraced it a long time ago!

The hours passed quickly, and the pilot announced that they would be landing soon! Carl made one last trip to the restroom to freshen up, wanting to look his best for Barbara. Immigration, customs, and baggage claim felt like a breeze since he was looking forward to something so sweet at the end of it all. As he walked towards the arrival lounge, he looked around for a familiar face. But he couldn't find Barbara anywhere. He paused and looked again. He checked his phone to see if there were any messages. There were none.

He was devastated. His eyes filled with tears and he felt like cursing Raj and his silly ideologies. Then he took a deep breath and started walking towards the taxi stand. As he walked, he replayed the moments he had shared with Barbara on Skype. He brushed his cheeks roughly to wipe away a few stray tears that had escaped, then reached into his breast pocket to retrieve a pair of tortoiseshell Ray-Ban sunglasses, throwing them over his tired, red eyes. He patted his pant pocket to check for his house keys. *Back to work, then, I guess*, he sighed. *It was a lovely dream while it lasted*. He tried to distract himself by focusing his mind on his business, thinking of his lawyer and wondering what transactions might have happened in his absence. Just then, he heard a screech, followed by a loud honk. "Carl!" someone yelled. He whipped around and squinted his eyes. He could not believe what he was seeing.

Carl removed his glasses and stared hard. A young man was running towards him, waving briskly. Tears began dripping down Carl's cheeks again. But, this time, Carl did not care. He let them fall. It was as if an emotional tap had just been turned on within him. All these years of repressed feelings and lack of communication had been begging for a release. The young man finally reached him, and they stood silently for a minute, looking each other in the eyes. The young man opened his mouth, but before he could say anything, Carl hugged him tightly. They both began crying uncontrollably. After a couple of emotional minutes, Carl began the conversation. "How have you been, Marx?"

"I am good, Dad." Carl's heart warmed at the sound of that word, which he had not heard uttered in so long. His son continued, "I heard from Mom that you were involved in a serious accident in a foreign country, and you were hurt very badly! How are you feeling now?" he asked earnestly, scanning Carl from head to toe. Marx had removed himself from his father's life after some grim and somber arguments over some of Carl's business deals, but upon hearing of the accident, he immediately regretted his harsh words and actions. The idea of losing his father for good made him realize that their differing opinions about the direction of the family business were not as big of a deal as they had seemed to him at the time.

Carl had been left alone in his palatial home, celebrating holiday after holiday by himself, until one day he received Raj's travel brochure. Hoping to live a happier life, he took a risk and decided to go on Raj's tour. Having his son in his arms, he knew that it had all been worth it. He no longer gave a damn about the accident or the physical harm it had inflicted upon him. Loose ligaments were a small price to pay for being reunited with one's family. "Oh, thank you my boy, but I am fine. There is some pain here and there, but it will heal soon."

Then Carl heard another loud honk, to which Marx quickly nodded and grabbed Carl's baggage while escorting him towards the honking car. Carl was surprised to see an old woman who was very stylishly dressed step out of the driver's seat. Barbara's glossy, perfectly styled brown hair was her crowning glory and Carl's weakness. She brushed her shiny hair aside as she removed her glasses and grabbed him. Her supple lips met his, and Carl was instantly transported to cloud nine. He wanted to stay like that forever, but then a traffic cop blew his whistle and yelled at them to get a move on. The couple waved in apology and quickly got into the car, giggling like teens. "I am so sorry for everything, Barbara." Carl confessed, looking deep into his ex-wife's eyes. Barbara and Marx apologized too as they pulled away from the curb, heading towards their own happy ending.

You and I

Lennard had already sent word to his friends and family about Darci's passing and expected that they would meet him at the airport when he arrived. He was looking forward to their support but dreading the difficult questions that would come along with it. Throughout his lengthy flight, he rehearsed his answers, hoping to make it easier on himself. Once the pilot announced their imminent landing, his heart started beating so fast that he thought he was having a heart attack. That made him nervous, and he began shouting for help. Passengers started freaking out and looked in his direction in helpless concern since they were all buckled up. The stewardess and the crew unleashed their seat belts and came running towards him. While one of them checked his vitals, the other fetched him a cup of water to help him calm down. Eventually, the water did the trick, and they all breathed a sigh of relief. They told him that it was merely a panic attack that he had suffered, not a heart attack.

The plane landed safely, and as Lennard patiently waited for Darci's body, his family members found him and gathered around. Most of them were crying uncontrollably, and that made him realize what he had actually lost. It made him very sorry for himself, and there was this little thing in his head that kept taking him to that moment when she was asking for another chance, and he was as quiet as a mouse. Raj's words echoed in his head, urging, Let it go! Let it go! Unexpected tears trickled down his cheeks as he thought of how stubborn he had been, unable to forgive Darci. Upon noticing Lennard cry, Darci's mom hugged him tight while consoling him, "You poor thing!" He did not have the heart to tell her mother the true reason why he was crying, so he hugged her tight and wept inconsolably. Seeing him in that state, his friends and relatives circled tighter around him, hugging him and trying their best to offer words of comfort or wisdom. Lennard took a while to calm down before accepting his cousin's offer of a ride home. Darci's body was taken to a morgue. Her parents had already arranged the burial ceremony.

Once he arrived at home, Lennard was struck by the sheer emptiness of their home. Darci had been like sunlight, filling their house with joyful noise and energy. *Why couldn't I just let it go?* Lennard berated himself. Darci's things were everywhere, as well as so many framed photos, showcasing their many adventures and happy moments together. Each smiling photo of Darci was like a needle that pierced Lennard to his core. He went into the kitchen, pulled open the knife drawer, and took out a knife. He stared at his wrist angrily, tears flowing down his cheeks. Then he remembered Raj's story. *A man is at his strongest when he is at rock bottom. Do I stand a chance of starting again?* Lennard wondered, letting the knife fall to the floor.

With a heavy heart, he left the kitchen and went to sit on his favorite velvet armchair. There was a beautiful sepia-tone portrait of Darci on the side table next to him, and he picked it up. He stared at it for a long time. He felt as if she was trying to tell him something. After a few minutes, he shook the portrait, crying out, "I am sorry! I am so very sorry, Darci!" he placed the photo back on the side table and fell to his knees before it, clasping his hands in a desperate plea. "I never meant for this to happen! Can you ever find it in your heart to forgive me?"

Just then, the picture fell towards him, and he quickly grabbed it. He hugged it to his chest, nodding as if had gotten the answer he was looking for. He lay in that position for some time and did not realize when sleep overtook his body. He was woken up by the sound of his phone ringing. He placed Darci's portrait respectfully back on the table and dusted himself off. It was the mortician calling, reminding Lennard to meet at the morgue with Darci's best clothes in order to get her ready for her final journey. Understandably, this shook him up, but his eyes were already tired and sore and he felt that he could not shed any more tears. He dragged himself to Darci's closet, where he took a minute to admire all of the colorful and frilly garments that she had worn on their special occasions. Finally, he forced himself to pull out her favorite dress. He had always marveled at her when she wore it. It was a maroon dress with lace trim along the border. It made her look beautiful and elegant and thinking back on his memories of her in it brought an unexpected smile to his face.

Cheered up by those warm memories, Lennard brewed a cup of coffee for himself and buttered a piece of toast. Then, without even thinking twice, he automatically made a pancake for her. "Breakfast is ready!" he shouted. As soon as the words left his lips, reality sunk back in, and he ate his breakfast in solemn, awful silence. He dressed himself, grabbed Darci's clothes, and headed to the church.

Darci's body was ready when he arrived. Lennard handed over the clothes and went to look around for a friendly face to help him get his mind off the pain, if even for a minute. He was surprised to see that there was a good turnout. The ceremony that her parents had planned was beautifully executed, bringing tears to every attendee's eyes. After another long and exhausting round of sobs and condolences, it was over. Lennard sat next to her grave long after all of the others left. Finally, at dusk, he went home, where he tucked her picture into bed with him and slept holding it.

The next day, he posted their apartment up for sale. Darci had decorated it beautifully, and it sold quickly as a result of that. He moved into a new, smaller place and donated most of Darci's things to the needy, taking only their photographs and his own possessions. He wanted to start fresh. He was grateful for the support of Raj's lively texts and useful bits of advice now and then. He looked forward to his new beginning, especially since age was by his side. Making sure to keep himself in check, this time, to avoid making the same mistakes again.

Story of My Life

Asha was glad to finally return to her apartment after such an exhausting ordeal. Kamala greeted her with a traditional bow, but Asha had been through so much that she simply pulled her caretaker close, embracing her as tightly as a long lost family member. Kamala was taken aback at first, but thinking of the accident and imagining everything that Asha must have gone through, she slowly wrapped her hands around her madam's shoulders. "How are you Kamala? I really missed you!" exclaimed Asha.

"I am well, and I have missed you too, madam!" replied Kamala with a smile.

When Asha had settled comfortably on her couch, Kamala brought her a glass of water and asked her about what had happened. Asha told Kamala everything, sparing no details. She raved and ranted about all of the crazy things that had happened, and all the fascinating and irritating people that she had met, and how each one of them had changed over the course of the trip. Kamala had never seen this side of her madam and, therefore, was spellbound by her tale. After Asha had finished her story, it was Kamala's turn to update her on everything that had occurred while Asha was away. Then Kamala served Asha her favorite food, which consisted of spicy potatoes with gravy and puffed whole wheat bread. Asha cleared her plate completely, even licking it off of her fingers. Finally, they both enjoyed a hot cup of tea.

Just then the phone rang. Her nods were quick and confident. As soon she put down the receiver, Asha settled down with her laptop and began typing fervently while flipping through the notes she had gathered during her trip.

"Madam, don't you want to rest?" inquired Kamala.

Asha peeped over the top of her glasses and replied, "I will Kamala... I will. But first, I must complete this document and send it off as soon as possible to the press so that justice can be done for a particular person."

That comment made Kamala curious since she wanted to know who will the master unveil to the world, but she knew better than to ask Asha questions about such matters. She set about unpacking Asha's bags and washing laundry as the sound of the clicking keyboard filled the air.

All of Me

After their successful peacemaking endeavor, Raj dropped an ecstatic Meera back at her apartment. When they conveyed the good news to Ira, she began jumping with joy. Meera showed her the wedding dress, which was well ironed and ready to be worn. Her mother had preserved the dress well, and she was delighted to wear it on her special day. "Wow, I love the skirt's color, and the top is such a perfect contrast! Plus, the gorgeous embroidery just makes it even more beautiful!" Ira squealed in delight while admiring the outfit. She delicately held the plastic garment bag, shifting it back and forth to see the way the sheen of the fabric glinted in the light.

"You can open it." Meera offered with a smile.

"Are you sure?"

"Yes, absolutely!" the soon-to-be-bride replied. So the plastic was shed, and both the women "oohed" and "ahhed" over the garment and its' delicate, sparkling embellishments.

"Okie Dokie, we shall meet later, I've got to go start cleaning up my apartment for my new bride's arrival!" Raj announced with a wink. Meera blushed.

"I can help you clean!" Ira volunteered cheerily.

Raj was thrilled to hear that since cleaning had never been his passion, but since courtesy demanded, he asked, "Are you sure?"

"Sure, I am free. How much television can I watch, after all?" she chuckled.

Raj clapped in delight, like a toddler who had just been handed a candy bar. Then the two of them left for Raj's place. Meera bid them a happy goodbye and headed out the door to get her dress altered.

Raj was a little anxious about taking his tourist to his small home, but then he realized that Ira was not just any tourist. After everything they had been through together, she was truly a friend. So he pushed his worries away and focused on his goal. To clean up! He unlocked the door, and cranked it open, allowing Ira to enter first, though he was still rubbing his hands together in despair, anticipating negative comments.

She took the first step in and stood still. "I like that enormous collage you have there!" she said, walking over to take a closer look.

"Aha! Those are all the postcards my ex-tourists send me now and then." he explained with glee. As Ira was admiring the photos, one particular card caught her eye. Only a quarter of it could be seen, since another postcard was partially covering it. She stared at it with incredible delight and couldn't resist reaching out to grab it. Ira was very curious about the addressee. As she pulled on the postcard, her hand slipped. Raj was stacking the old newspapers in a corner when he heard a loud bang. He quickly turned to see Ira surrounded by a swarm of fluttering postcards. The frame had fallen down, freeing all of its contents. Ira sputtered apologies and looked as if she might cry. Raj just laughed and shook his head over her clumsiness. "Nah! No worries! This was bound to come down one day or another! Meera always warned me that it was getting too heavy, but I kept procrastinating!" Raj chuckled as he bent down to pick up the cards.

Ira nodded, still captivated by the thought of that one postcard, which had borne a picture of her hometown. All she could think about was that picture, but now she couldn't spot that particular card due to the mess she had made. She brushed her hair away from her eyes, and said, "Well, all the more reason to clean up now!" They both started picking up the scattered cards, and soon the postcards were stacked on his table. Raj took the few that remained in the old and cracked wooden frame and handed them to Ira. "Tea?" he offered. Ira was so anxious to find that one card, that she refused his offer of tea even though it sounded delicious. Raj was pleased to see her dedication, not knowing what actually was going on her mind. He left her to sort the postcards and began working on a stack of magazines. Suddenly Ira exclaimed, "Aha!" Raj hurried over to see what she was looking at. She was reading the postcard from her hometown with a frown. She held up the note towards Raj so he could read it. "This name sounds familiar…" she said, looking at Raj.

Raj took the card from her outstretched hand and read the name of the addressee. "Oh, Edwin! Edwin Garmin! He is a sweet guy. He definitely had some serious issues when he came to me, but am glad he is enjoying himself now, no matter what! Do you know him?"

"He is from my town! And did you know that a man by the name of Edwin Garmin saved my life? It might very well be the same man!" Ira's eyes were wide. She had been dying to discover more about the mysterious man who had saved her. She even had a hunch that it might lead to a happy ending of her own. The fact that finding Edwin might give her happiness made her, even more, distressed since she wanted that feeling so badly in her life. "Tell me more about this guy, Raj!" she pleaded with clasped hands and desperate puppy dog eyes, since she knew the guide was a real professional when it came to talking about his tourists' secrets.

Raj swayed his head from left to right, refusing with a smile. Seeing her devastated expression, he added an apology.

Ira was only getting started, though. She continued her plea, saying; "You see this mark on my wrist. I did this to myself when Pete left me! Then this guy by the name of Ed Garmin rescued me, and he took me to the hospital."

"Wow! You are a brave lady." Raj commended her without being judgmental.

"Just brave?" she asked while continuing to sob. "You just don't understand, I have to find this man!" she began pacing in circles, pounding her left fist against her right palm. "When the nurse told me

I was rescued by him, I got no vibes. I had no idea how or where to find him… but now… now I have to find him since I have a strong feeling that it will lead me to my happiness. Please, please Raj, tell me where to find him?" she pleaded.

Her desperate plea left the empathetic Raj in a pickle, and he didn't know how to respond.

Then Ira snapped her fingers energetically. She began to rummage inside her purse pockets.

"What are you looking for?" inquired Raj.

"You know, I just might be able to connect the dots myself!" answered Ira.

"The nurse had mentioned that this guy lived in my building. Unfortunately, I was not in the right frame of mind to investigate his whereabouts, until now." She grabbed her phone and texted her building administrator in Seattle. Raj was full of anticipation but kept a straight face. "Within a few minutes, I should know exactly where Edwin Garmin lives in my building!" she squealed triumphantly.

Raj sat down and crossed his arms in thought. "It is quite early for your building administrator to text you that information, don't you think?"

"What do you mean?" asked Ira as she pulled her long blonde hair into a bun and sat down across him.

Raj drew a deep breath and uttered, "Ed lives extremely close to you. In fact, he has had a bit of a crush on you ever since you and Pete moved into that building. He did other favors for you before this latest one, but you were too wrapped up in your own life to notice." he stated bluntly.

This was the first time that Ira had seen so much attitude from Raj, and she was suddenly filled with guilt. "What do you mean?"

Raj paused, looking down at the floor. He sighed and confessed that it was most definitely Ira's Edwin who had visited him, and that his tour had helped Edwin realize that he needed to get over Ira, since he likely would never have a chance with her. "After he did that final favor for you, he slid my brochure under your door." Raj finished with a sad smile. "See, Ira, I have known about you for a long time. Edwin is a kind man who showed so much concern for your wellbeing, even though you never even gave him a second glance. Ira Addison, you are a lucky girl! And the sad part is that you were never even aware of it. All you did was feel sorry for yourself and take advantage of the attention from my Peter, even though a spark for something deeper was waiting right across the hall from you."

Ira was in tears. "How soon can I get a ticket back home?" she asked.

"Excuse me? I thought you were going to be Meera's bridesmaid? You would just ditch us like that, for him?" he said with a sly smile and a twinkle of mischief in his eyes.

At first, Ira was taken aback, but then after reading the mischievous expression on his face, she laughed and hugged him tight. "This journey has definitely unraveled new beginnings for me!"

"Don't forget about Peter too!" Raj was quick to add. "The past few weeks have opened a whole new chapter for him as well." Upon hearing his name, Ira grew solemn and expressed her wishes for his speedy and complete recovery.

A few productive hours went by as they cleaned Raj's place and arranged his belongings to make room for Meera to move in. Raj's phone beeped and he picked it up thinking it was Meera who had texted. Instead, he raised one eyebrow upon reading it, then extended the screen towards Ira, who leaned forward with curiosity. Then her complexion flushed bright red. She bit her lip and typed something with a pensive tilt of her head. Then she clicked the send button, and with a content expression, handed the phone back to Raj.

Raj could not resist. "So, are you happy now? You finally connected with him!"

"Indeed!" Ira beamed. "Now, chop-chop! Let's finish getting this all sorted out! You are getting married tomorrow!" Raj laughed and they resumed their work.

A couple hours later, Raj dropped Ira back at Meera's house. Raj got a quick glimpse of his bride to be and winked at her. Her mother was there as well, applying henna tattoos to Meera's skin, per Hindu tradition. Raj left the three women to enjoy their female bonding time and headed home to groom himself for his big day and get some shuteye.

The next day was an ordinary Sunday for many, but not for a particular soon-to-be-married couple. All of the wedding participants milled about in joyful chaos, making the necessary last-minute preparations. By mid-morning, they met at the temple, where some of their friends were already waiting. The bride and groom were both garbed in richly hued traditional Indian marriage clothing, and Ira was thrilled to be sporting a flowy aquamarine tunic and matching pants, also known as "salwar kameez" from Meera's own wardrobe. The marriage was conducted in a Hindu traditional way, in which the couple circled a fire while making promises to each other to be there in times of crisis and happiness. Meera's mother was sniffing quietly, and Ira had tears rolling down her face as she admired the touching ritual. Ira was mesmerized by the chants of the priest, and the vows and the mutual nods made by the couple. She marveled at the beauty of the rituals that keep humans grounded, no matter what country we are from or what our ethnic background is. Deep in her heart, Ira longed to go home, since she now knew that someone was waiting for her. At the conclusion of the ceremony, flowers were showered upon the new couple, and then the elders blessed them. A couple of Meera's friends presented her with a gift certificate, and she squealed with delight, hugging her friends tightly. "Guess what, Raj? We get to spend a few nights in The Taj, courtesy of my fellow hospitality employees!" Raj was impressed and thanked Meera's friends graciously.

After having lunch with everyone, the newlyweds headed to Meera's apartment to help sort her bags and deliver them to Raj's home. Then they helped Ira finish packing and dropped her off at the airport. There were lots of hugs, lots of giggles, and lots of teary eyes between the girls while Raj kept his composure and a steady smile. "Keep in touch!" he requested when she was about to leave for boarding.

"Thank you Raj," she whispered back as she hugged him. "For everything." She smiled graciously, then added with a wink, "And, if by any chance, Edwin and I ever get married, you two will be invited as guests of honor!" They all laughed heartily as she headed off towards her boarding gate.

After that long day, the couple headed to the Taj Hotel to enjoy their first night together as man and wife. However, they were accosted by a mob of strangers flashing their cameras at them in the lobby. They were taken aback, and confused. They ran up to their hotel room and quickly slammed the door behind themselves before any more pictures could be taken. "What is going on?" Meera exclaimed.

"I have not the slightest clue!" replied Raj with a confused shrug.

Then Meera got a picture message from one of her girlfriends. It was an image of an article in the Sunday paper, titled "Voyagers Into the Unknown: How A Local Tour Company Is Changing Lives." The report contained pictures of Raj, his company logo, and many fantastic and unusual details about how his work had impacted people worldwide.

"Well, that explains the paparazzi!" Meera exclaimed, thumping her husband on the back proudly. "Congratulations! I can't wait to brag about you even more now!" she winked cheekily. Raj was a local celebrity now, and now that Meera was "Mrs. Malhotra" she could enjoy the perks and bragging rights. "I wonder who wrote it, though…" Meera peered at the photo, using her fingers to zoom in on the touchscreen display. "No way!"

"Huh?" asked a confused Raj.

"Asha!" cried Meera.

"Asha what?"

"She was actually a reporter who was just posing as a tourist, and this article is written by her!"

"I don't believe it! Why did she have to keep it a secret?" Raj wondered aloud as Meera rolled her eyes. Meera beamed at the sight of a complimentary honeymoon fruit basket and bottle of champagne. She popped the bottle joyfully.

"That's one more thing to celebrate! Cheers, honey!" Meera extended a sparkling flute of champagne to Raj, but he was lost in deep thought.

"People visited me when they were at rock bottom. I helped them change for the better, and that's why I was successful."

"Sure, and you are good at it! Why the long face? What's the problem?"

Raj took the champagne flute from her hand and stared down at it with a melancholy expression. "The problem is that I won't be able to deliver that kind of same success to the general public."

"What's not to deliver? You are a wonderful person. You are great at what you do. So what could stand in between you and your new clients?"

"It's the pressure, and the expectations!" Raj admitted. "Meera, if someone is declared famous, their work is always critically acclaimed, which is fine, but it is not I who will be doing the job. I doubt that many people will understand what I mean by that." He paused and continued, "You see, I am not a 'magician' like how the article said. I am just a mere man giving the basic knowledge of survival to men and women who are in search of happiness."

"I understand!" Meera nodded in agreement and picked up Raj's phone. She dialed Asha's number and handed it to Raj. "Why don't you try talking to her and getting a better explanation."

Raj agreed, and soon he was deep in conversation with Asha. Meera watched his expressions intently throughout the conversation, and it seemed promising. "So? What did she say?" Meera asked eagerly as soon as he hung up.

Raj sighed, "She said she believed in me more than I believe in myself."

"Well isn't that something!" Meera smiled and kissed him gently on the cheek. Then she raised her glass, indicating for him to do the same. "Here's to a new beginning!"

Raj reluctantly complied, still looking unsure. Meera saw his expression and took his hand, intertwining her fingers with his. "Don't stress, Raj. Just take this as an exciting new challenge! Plus, you are your own boss, so you can still feel free to choose your customers according to what you feel comfortable with!"

Raj nodded, finally seeing the silver lining and letting his mind open up to the positive possibilities of what the article might bring. He smiled, and then their celebration began! Laughter was soon accompanied by passion, and they fell into a wonderland of lust that turned into love. The hotel room was their home for a couple of nights. All they did was order room service and let passion fill their days and nights. In the midst of it, Raj was pleased to receive many congratulatory texts and emails from past clients. His favorite messages were the ones from his latest flock of birds. Ira let the couple know of her safe arrival back home, and her plans to meet Edwin on arrival. Asha sent the couple some warm words of marriage advice that she had learned over the years, and Carl sent them a gift basket heaping with snacks, which ended up coming in quite handy for vital energy in-between their room service deliveries.

Part of Me

When Ira boarded her flight to Seattle, her restlessness was in a different form than it had been when she departed for India. Thankfully, there was nobody to judge her during her flight home since the seat beside her was empty. She had space to spread out, and she let her mind focus on how to address Edwin. Just thinking about the possibility of a new romance gave her goose bumps. It was all so exciting and mysterious! She had no clue what Edwin looked like, and she was hoping that he would be the handsome and dashing man of her dreams, however after everything she had been through, she knew that looks were secondary to personality. She was banking on emotional support and a good sense of humor.

For a moment, Ira was surprised by her sudden leap in maturity, but then after pondering the past few weeks, she wasn't so surprised. She had touched the sky and was grateful to touch the ground again after all of the nerve wrecking drama. Now she knew that there was solace in the dirt, and even though her hands got muddy, and her hair dusty, there was unexpected beauty and comfort to be found. Her thoughts helped the flight to pass by quickly, and her airplane landed even sooner than she was expecting. As the plane rolled towards the gate, she looked out her window and noticed that her heart fluttered with excitement and hope. It no longer ached the way it had when she left the country. Ira was pleased with the changes that she noticed in herself and was excited to see what the future might have in store for her.

After going through customs and picking up her bags, Ira headed to the bathroom to freshen up. She combed her long champagne-colored hair and reapplied her lipstick. She had a gut feeling that Edwin might be the key to what was missing in her life. They had only exchanged a few texts prior to boarding, but she felt like they already shared a special connection. She paused at the edge of the pickup lane in front of the baggage claim exit, scanning the faces in the crowd. Her feet were so firmly rooted to the ground that even if she had tried to call for a taxi, she had a feeling that they would not have budged. Her heart told her to wait for him, but her brain told her to just be practical and get into a cab. The confusion within her must have shown on her face since more than a couple travelers paused to ask her if she was okay. Her subconscious mind was so stubborn that it was controlling her body while the conscious mind wanted to let go. She teetered on the edge of the curb near the crosswalk, trying to decide whether to cross the street to the taxi stand or to continue waiting on the curb for Edwin. Another traveler brushed past her in a hurry, knocking her off balance. She was so engrossed in her thoughts that even as she fell forward, she failed to notice a car that was pulling up at the same time, and which nearly hit her. The loud screech of the brakes awoke her senses, and she slammed her palm angrily on the hood of the Toyota Prius and cursed, adding, "Damn these hybrid cars, they can creep up on you like a demon!"

"I am so sorry to keep you waiting!" cried the driver, as he opened his door and stepped towards her. "I hope you did not have to wait too long?" Confused, Ira spun around her to see who he was talking to, but no one seemed to be paying him any mind. *Could he be talking to her? Was it really Edwin?* She scanned him from head to toe. He was a lanky man with earnest black-brown eyes, a French beard, and shiny brown hair. He looked sharp and scholarly in a navy blazer and crisp khaki pants. He stopped directly in front of her, extending his right hand towards hers. *Edwin. Finally!* "Hey, how are you?" he asked with a nervous smile.

Ira hesitated at first, "Err... I am... fine," she mumbled, smiling. But when she looked into his warm brown eyes, something made her feel much more at ease. Her smile widened, and she confidently flipped her gleaming golden hair, hoping that he would notice.

"May I?" he requested, gesturing to her luggage.

"Absolutely!" Ira beamed. He loaded her luggage into his Prius, opened her door in a gentlemanly manner, and soon they were silently rolling away.

"I am genuinely sorry for being so late! My meeting at work ran later than I expected," he confessed.

Ira didn't care why he was late. All that mattered was that he was here now. She looked at the man behind the wheel and a glimmer of recognition sparked in her brain. She had seen his face before... in the elevator a few times, and in the mail room. "I *do* remember you! You live one floor above me, right?"

"Yes!" Edwin replied, clearly thrilled that she did have some recollection of him after all. "I am that dull, average-looking guy!" he joked.

That comment made Ira's face red, and she looked out the window, trying to hide her embarrassment over having been so self-absorbed. She suddenly recalled a particular incident, when she, Pete, and Edwin had been in the elevator, and Pete had noticed her eyeing Edwin. He had immediately called her out on it, even though Edwin was trapped in there with them. They argued the whole way down and Edwin was quick to exit the elevator the minute it touched the ground floor.

Ira sighed, and then turned to face Edwin. "I am very sorry... I should have been nicer to you."

"Nah! Don't worry about it! I was just kidding! You're gorgeous! Of course, you wouldn't think much of a guy like me."

"Oh! Edwin... by just seeing you, I have not only connected all the dots but have been able to solve the whole puzzle. I just wish I had figured it out sooner." she said, tucking a few strands of hair behind her right ear. "Thank you for saving my life! The nurse told me your name, but I was too full of myself back then..." she said while gently placing her left hand over his right hand. Touching him was important to her since she wanted to convey how genuine her feelings were, especially after her arrogant past.

Prior to going home, they stopped at a coffee shop to rewind and laugh about the times when they had bumped into each other randomly. There was the time that she dropped a parcel and he picked it up and gave it to her. Another time, she carelessly spilled her coffee in the lobby on her way to work and he had silently wiped it up without a word. Each encounter was completely meaningless to Ira back then, but they were treasured memories to Edwin. Ira humbly apologized for all of her insensitive acts, while Edwin embraced her with open arms. Before leaving, they toasted with their coffee mugs to a new beginning, and hand-in-hand they promised to be there for each other from that point on, whether it be as friends, or something more. For love to happen, they would have to first start off by liking each other and would need to find common ground. *Would they prefer a dog or a cat? A house or an apartment? One child, or four? Cooking at home, or going to a restaurant?* If they could first straighten out the essential things, they might have a chance of someday being happily married. Ira needed time to unwind within while being assured by Edwin that things could change for the better if she was ready to take a step forward. Even though she had been cold to him before, Edwin knew that during their previous encounters she had been trapped in a bad relationship, so he gave her the benefit of the doubt. He hoped to erase the ugliness of the past and start anew.

Set Fire to the Rain

After their honeymoon, Raj and Meera were excited to begin their new lives. The newlyweds were getting familiarized with each other's living patterns and focused on making the necessary adjustments to prevent getting in each other's ways. They both realized that adaptation was necessary for their new journey to begin, and they tried to go as easy on each other as possible. They embraced each other's flaws, instead of getting upset about a dirty dish in the sink here, or an unfolded piece of laundry over there.

At work, Raj opened his email folder to find a plethora of emails from prospective clients who hoped to begin a new chapter of their lives by touring a city with such a rich history of love and hope. Thanks to Asha's article getting published in such a reputable paper, his already positive reputation had skyrocketed. Raj scanned each of their emails, taking notes and grouping them under various dates. Then he sent out a questionnaire to each of the prospective tourists, to determine whether they would be a good fit for his services.

All of the humanity is suffering from one big problem, and that is a loss. However, all of us strive for one big goal as well, and that is happiness. Keeping that in mind and focusing on positive thoughts, he started making arrangements for his upcoming tour. He planned to take his tourists along the roads of Agra, visiting monuments that were decades old, but yet still spoke to each visitor in the universal language of humanity. This would allow the new birds to embrace their misfortune and transcribe the many folds within themselves that lay hidden, either due to ignorance or just their fast-paced lifestyles.

Raj vowed that he would find a way to help each of his tourists discover the hidden potential within themselves, by giving them practical tools instead of empty theory and rhetoric. He had no fancy degree or formal training for this, only the gift of his own personal experiences and struggles. He had learned how to maneuver the curveballs that life throws by falling, getting hurt, putting himself back together, and getting up again to face life. That was the baton that he loved passing along to his visitors. In return, he gained valuable knowledge and insight from his visitors about other cultures, other languages, and most importantly, other personalities. There was never a dull moment during a day at Raj Touristry. The sun was rising outside of his window and birds were chirping in the already-warm morning air. A flock of birds flew past Raj's window and he smiled as he thought of the many birds whom he had guided and the many more which were to come.

Printed in the United States
By Bookmasters